SCOTS
in
LATIN AMERICA

by
David Dobson

CLEARFIELD

Printed for
Clearfield Company, Inc. by
Genealogical Publishing Co., Inc.
Baltimore, Maryland
2003

International Standard Book Number: 0-8063-5202-7

INTRODUCTION

Scottish links with what has come to be known as Latin America date back to the sixteenth century and thus predate any links with or settlement by Scots in North America and the West Indies.

The earliest Scot known to have settled in Latin America was a Thomas Blake or Black, a merchant possibly from Aberdeen, who moved via Spain to Mexico City in the early sixteenth century. He accompanied Coronado on his expedition over what is now the American Southwest in 1540. About the same time a group of French Huguenots from Rouen settled on a site now known as Rio de Janeiro but were driven out in due course by the Portuguese who had a prior claim to the area. Among these French settlers was a group of Scottish soldiers of fortune who had been recruited to defend the colony. During the latter half of the seventeenth century, there was a handful of Scots living among the English and Dutch settlers in Surinam, some of whom later moved north to the West Indies. Scottish records indicate at least three voyages from Scotland to Surinam during the seventeenth century. Between 1698 and 1699, an unsuccessful attempt was made to settle 3,000 Scots at Darien on the Isthmus of Panama. Details on many of these emigrants can be found in my *The Original Scots Colonists of Early America: Caribbean Supplement, 1611-1707 [GPC, Baltimore, 1999]*. This volume concentrates on Scots known to have settled on the mainland of Central America and South America during the nineteenth century but does list a handful of earlier emigrants.

Emigration from Scotland to Latin America only began in earnest once the power of Spain in the hemisphere began to wane. In the later eighteenth century, there were locations such as the Bay of Honduras or Surinam where British and Dutch planters and merchants had settled which were virtually the only places for Scots until the Wars of Liberation during the early nineteenth century removed the restrictions on immigration imposed by Spain. After the end of the Napoleonic Wars in 1815, substantial numbers of demobilised soldiers and sailors, including many Scots, flocked to South America to aid the revolutionaries in their fight for liberty from Spain. Once that was achieved, emigration and investment occurred. Soon Scottish newspapers were reporting shiploads of emigrants bound for South America, for example in 1825 the <u>Norval</u>, the <u>Symetry</u> and the <u>Harmony</u> set sail for Argentina with bricklayers, implement makers, blacksmiths, miners, quarries and especially farmers. British merchant houses, banks, railway companies, mining companies, industrialists, planters and ranchers became established throughout Latin America and brought with them skilled workers and professionals from all over the British Isles. This book, while not definitive, identifies many of the Scots who settled throughout Latin America from Mexico to Argentina during the nineteenth century and is based on primary source material in Scotland, especially documents in archives, newspapers and monumental inscriptions.

David Dobson
St Andrews, Scotland,
2002.

SCOTS IN LATIN AMERICA
1800-1899

ABERCROMBY, GEORGE, a doctor in Mexico around 1770, brother of Sir George Abercromby of Birkenbog, and father of John, an officer in the Spanish Army, and of Mary Louise. [NAS.NRAS#0002]

ADAM, JOHN, born in Dingwall during 1883, died in Buenos Ayres in 1907. [Dingwall, St Clement's, g/s]

ADAMS, RICHARD, born 1793, an architect, wife Anna and four children, emigrated from Leith to Buenos Ayres on the Symmetry, master William Cochrane, on 22 May 1825, landed there on 11 August 1825. [SRP#18]

ADAMSON, JAMES GREY, born 1840, from Leven, Fife, an engineer of the Antofagusta Nitrate Works in Chile, died in Valparaiso on 14 May 1881. [FFP]; cnf 25 February 1882 Edinburgh. [NAS.SC70.1.1/833][S#11,844]

ADAMSON, JAMES GRAY, son of the above, born 1878, died in Mexico City on 27 February 1903. [FH]

ADAMSON, ..., daughter of J. G. Adamson, was born at Sarapaca Nitrate Company Works, La Novica, Iquilos, Peru, 18 July 1868. [S#7824]

ADAMSON, ..., son of engineer Robert Adamson, was born in Rio de Janeiro on 31 July 1868. [S#7843]

ADAMSON, ..., son of James G. Adamson, managing engineer of the Salav Works, was born in Antofagasta, Bolivia, on 5 February 1878. [S#10,816]

AIKMAN,....., son of W.G.Aikman, was born in Belize, British Honduras, on 11 June 1882. [S#12,155]

AIRD, ANNE, born 1806, a servant, emigrated from Leith to Buenos Ayres on the Symmetry, master William Cochrane, on 22 May 1825, landed there on 11 August 1825. [SRP#18]; Anne Aird born 1824, daughter of Thomas Aird and .... Young in Alloway, Ayrshire, died in Buenos Ayres 28 February 1828. [Alloway g/s]

AIRD, JAMES, born 1797, a carpenter, with his wife Mary and one child emigrated from Leith to Buenos Ayres on the Symmetry, master William Cochrane, on 22 May 1825, landed there on 11 August 1825. [SRP#18]

AITCHISON, WILLIAM PATERSON, cashier of the Brazilian Mining Association of London, died in Gongo Souca, Brazil, on 5 January 1832. [AJ#4399][EEC#18793]

AITKEN, DAVID, born 1826, son of Andrew Aitken and Hannah Kinlyside, died in Rio de Janeiro on 24 November 1861. [Cockburnspath g/s, Berwickshire]

AITKEN, JOHN GEORGE, son of John Aitken a physician in Edinburgh, died in Demerara on 3 August 1803. [DPCA#73][AJ#2919]

ALISON, JOHN, born in Paisley, Renfrewshire, on 19 January 1839, died in Callao on 2 May 1868. [Woodside g/s, Paisley]

ALLAN, COLIN, MD, died in Demerara in 1805. [SM#68/565][AJ#2991]

ALLAN, JAMES, married Jane, second daughter of John Ord, Redhall, Morayshire, at Plantation William, Demerara, on 21 February 1826. [AJ#4089]

ALLAN, JAMES, Captain of the Thomas of Glasgow, son of James Allan a watchmaker in Aberdeen, died in Demerara on 10 September 1841. [AJ:17.11.1841]

ALLAN, JOHN, born 1728, son of Hugh Allan a merchant in Kilmarnock, Ayrshire, died in Surinam during 1813. [EA#5194/13]

ALLAN, JOHN, born in Edinburgh before 1815, son of Francis Allan and Isabella Sheach, died in Peru. [Old Calton g/s, Edinburgh]

ALLAN, JOHN SCOTT, born 1840, son of Hugh Allan [1808-1859] and Janet Scott [1802-1896], died in Buenos Ayres 26 September 1897. [Ballantrae g/s, Ayrshire]

ALLAN, THOMAS, late of Society, South Queensferry, West Lothian, died in Lima, Peru, 2 August 1862. [S#2261]

ALLAN, WILLIAM, born in 1850, from Auchenblae, died in Georgetown, Demerara, on 10 October 1881. [AJ:19.11.1881]

ALLAN, WILLIAM, born in 1877, late of the Town and County Bank in Aberdeen, only son of William Allan, Rowan Bank, Peterculter, Aberdeenshire, an overseer on Plantation Uitolugt, Demerara, died on 22 August 1899. [AJ:18.9.1899]

ALLISON, DAVID, eldest son of Andrew Allison in Glasgow, died in Valparaiso, Chile, 25 March 1870. [S#8359]; cnf 1871 Edinburgh. [NAS.SC70.1.153/538]

ALSTEIN, FREDERICK A M, born 1815, died in Demerara on 9 March 1860. [Dean g/s Edinburgh]

ALSTEIN, FREDERICK ROBERT, born 1842, son of Frederick A. M. Alstein and Janet M. Alstein, died in Demerara on 13 March 1866. [Dean g/s, Edinburgh]

ALVES, JAMES STEWART, in Demerara then in Lugton, inv.16 June 1813 Edinburgh. [NAS.SC70.1.8.303]

AMOS, ANNIE, wife of William Mitchell, from Aberdeen, died in Quilmos, Buenos Ayres, on 19 February 1890. [AJ:19.4.1890]

ANDERSON, DAVID, only son of David Anderson a merchant in Dundee, died in Curacao on his arrival from Monte Video on 30 November 1807. [SM#70/317]

ANDERSON, DAVID, born 1775, a farmer, with his wife Mary and two children emigrated from Leith to Buenos Ayres on the Symmetry master William Cochrane, on 22 May 1825, landed there on 11 August 1825. [SRP#18]

ANDERSON, HARRY G., a broker in Monte Video, 1891. [NAS.RS.Forfar.50.274]

ANDERSON, JAMES, born in Stonykirk on 5 November 1821, son of Reverend James Anderson and Mary McGhie, a vine grower, died in Valparaiso, Chile. [F#2/355]

ANDERSON, JAMES R., an engineer in Valparaiso, Chile, 1899. [NAS.RS.Forfar.53.21]

ANDERSON, JANET STORY, wife of Reverend Francis Forbes minister of St Luke's in British Guiana, died on the Plantation de Willem on 9 March 1847. [EEC#21493]

ANDERSON, Reverend JOHN, born in Nairnshire, educated at the universities of Edinburgh and Aberdeen, minister of a Presbyterian Church in New Amsterdam, British Guiana, 1835, died there on 6 July 1840. [AJ#4834][F.7.673]

ANDERSON, JOHN, born in 1781, son of John Anderson, farmer in Easter Buchanty, and Ann Moir (1750-1801), died in Honduras in March 1813. [Monzie g/s]

ANDERSON, JOHN IZATT, of the Otago Government in New Zealand, son of John Anderson, late in Mexico, died 30 October 1866. [S#7322]

ANDERSON, MARGARET, born 1840, wife of William Anderson, died in Buenos Ayres on 30 December 1873. [S#9534]

ANDERSON, STEPHEN, a surgeon in Pisco, South America, serviced as heir to his father John Anderson a manufacturer in Lanark, on 5 May 1826. [NAS.S/H]

ANDERSON, WILLIAM, eldest son of John Anderson a merchant in Leith, in Augustura, Guayana province, Venezuela, in 1819. [NAS.RD5.166.130]

ANDERSON, ..., son of Peter Anderson and his wife ..... Lindsay from Dundee, was born in Fabrica de Gas, Santiago, Chile, on 24 June 1877. [EC#28980]

ANDERSON, ..., son of Walter Anderson, was born in Rio de Janeiro, on 17 December 1877. [EC#29117]

ANDREW, Mrs ELIZABETH, daughter of Andrew Millar, Writer to the Signet, wife of Richard J. Andrew a merchant in Belize, died in Belize, Honduras, on 19 March 1831. [EEC#18646]

ANDREW, RICHARD JAMES, died in Belize, Honduras, on 13 February 1832. [EEC#18782]

ANDREWS, DAVID, born 1854, fourth son of Peter Andrews in Leith, died in Chile in 1882. [S#12,081]

ANGUS, BELL, born 1894, fourth daughter of David Angus, died in Colico, Chile, on 6 January 1899. [S#17359]

ARMSTRONG, JAMES, born 1831, died in Buenos Ayres in 1871. [SRP#365]

ARNOTT, GEOFFREY LEITH, born 9 March 1865, son of Arthur Philip Arnott and his wife Margaret, died at Bahia Blancs, Argentina, 15 September 1910. [Dean g/s. Edinburgh]

ARTHUR, GEORGE, in Lima, Peru, 1889, son of George Archer, a cooper in Leith, and his wife Janet Bryce. [NAS.SH.17.9.1889]

ARTHUR, JAMES INNES, born 22 July 1785, son of Reverend Robert Arthur and Ann Munro in Resolis, settled in Demerara, died at sea on 20 August 1816. [F#6/19]

ARTHUR, LAUCHLAN, late of Bo'ness, West Lothian, assistant secretary of the Hand-in-Hand Insurance Company, died in Georgetown, Demerara, on 29 August 1881. [S#11,919]

ARTHUR, ROBERT, late of Berbice, fifth son of Reverend Robert Arthur of Resolis, died in Cromarty on 3 July 1829. [S#994]

ARTHUR, WILLIAM, born 1799, a cooper, with his wife Margaret and one child, emigrated from Leith to Buenos Ayres on the Symmetry on 22 May 1825, landed there on 11 August 1825. [SRP#18]

ASTLEY, CHARLES JOSEPH, a merchant in Pernambuco, Brazil, brother of Thomas Astley a chemist in Musselburgh, 1851. [NAS.S/H.1851][NAS.RD5.867.590]

ATTWELL, WILLIAM, born 1782, a basket maker, with his wife Agnes and five children, emigrated from Leith to Buenos Ayres on the Symmetry, master William Cochrane, on 22 May 1825, landed there on 11 August 1825. [SRP#18]

AULD, ALEXANDER, of Carcoside, late a planter in Demerara, cnf 1 May 1821 Dumfries, father of Matilda. [NAS.PS3.14.383]

AULD, ROBERT OGILVIE, born 1806, second son of Robert Auld, Crane Court, London, died in Guanesevi, Durango, Mexico, on 30 October 1846. [EEC#21451]

AUSTINE, ALEXANDER, son of George Austine of Torwood, died in Berbice on 20 September 1843. [AJ#5053]

AUSTINE, JAMES, eldest son of Mr Austine the postmaster of Fettercairn, Kincardineshire, died in Windsor Forest, Demerara, on 2 August 1839. [AJ#4787]

BAILLIE, JOHN, a surgeon in Demerara, 13 April 1824. [NAS.RD#394/383]; a surgeon in Edinburgh late in Demerara, died 12 August 1829. Cnf Edinburgh 1830

BAILLIE, SUTTIE, late in Edinburgh, died in Demerara during 1801. [AJ#2825]

BAIRD, HUGH, son of Thomas Baird a merchant in Kilmarnock, Ayrshire, a merchant in Rio de Janeiro around 1845. [NAS.S/H]

BAIRD, ROBERT, a merchant in Surinam by May 1689. [NAS.RH1.2.772/3]

BAIRD, WILLIAM, born 1846, died in Valparaiso on 24 April 1878. [South Dalziel g/s]

BALD, ROBERT, born 1842, second son of John Bald in Wells, Roxburghshire, died on Estancia Rosario, Buenos Ayres, on 22 January 1870. [S#8299]

BALFOUR, ..., son of James Balfour, was born in Valparaiso on 6 February 1874. [S#9576]

BALGARNIE, MARION AITKEN, daughter of William Balgarnie, died in Windsor Villa, Demerara, on 21 January 1872. [S#8910]

BALGARNIE, WILLIAM, a merchant, married Marion Mitchell, second daughter of John Howden of Nether Braco, Perthshire, at Windsor Villa, Georgetown, Demerara, 15 November 1870. [S#8545]

BALGARNIE, WILLIAM, born 1846, from Edinburgh, died in Georgetown, Demerara, on 31 July 1873. [S#9388]

BALGARNIE, ..., daughter of William Balgarnie, was born in Valparaiso on 27 August 1871. [S#8804]

BANKS, BESSIE, born 1847, third daughter of John Banks, 50 South Bridge, Edinburgh, died in Belize on 29 August 1869. [S#8164]

BANKS, WALTER, born in Edinburgh 1838, died in Rosario de Sante Fe on 25 January 1869. [S#8002]

BARBER, MARGARET, born 1800, a servant, emigrated from Leith to Buenos Ayres on the Symmetry on 22 May 1825, landed there on 11 August 1825. [SRP#18]

BARBOUR, Reverend JOHN, MA, minister of St Saviour's, Berbice, died at Ormond Villa, Berbice, on 12 October 1861. [S#2002][F.7.679]

BARBOUR, ROBERT, born in 1799, late a merchant in Buenos Ayres, died in Liverpool on 6 November 1849. [Woodside g/s, Paisley]

BARCLAY, ROBERT, a surgeon in Buenos Ayres, dead by 1739. [NAS.S/H]

BARCLAY, ROBERT, born 1802, a servant, with his wife Helen and one child, emigrated from Leith to Buenos Ayres on the Symmetry, master William Cochrane, on 22 May 1825, landed there on 11 August 1825. [SRP#18]

BARKER, JONATHAN, born 1785, a bricklayer, with his wife Elizabeth and two children, emigrated from Leith to Buenos Ayres on the Symmetry, master William Cochrane, on 22 May 1825, landed there on 11 August 1825. [SRP#18]

BARKER, QUINTIN MCADAM, born in Bridgend, Sanquhar, Dumfriesshire, during 1804, son of Thomas Barker and Sarah Johnston, a wine merchant who died in Rio de Janeiro on 2 December 1839. [Sanquhar g/s, Dumfriesshire]

BARNES, PHILIP EDWARD, Danish Consul at Coquimbo, Chile, died on 2 October 1860. [EEC#23559]

BARNHILL, WILLIAM, born in Glasgow 1826, son of James Barnhill a merchant, educated at Glasgow University, minister of St Clement's parish, Berbice, 1879-1883, died in Berbice on 22 October 1883. [F.3/225]

BARR, ALEXANDER, born 1855, son of John Barr and Rosanna McColgan, died Rio de Janeiro 15 March 1886. [Lennoxtown g/s]

BARR, ROBERT, son of James Barr in Port Glasgow, a merchant in Demerara around 1803. [NAS.S/H]

BARR, ..., daughter of A. Barr, was born in Georgetown, Demerara, on 18 March 1881. [S#11,776]

BARRIE, WILLIAM PARISH ROBERTSON, only son of William Barrie in Dalkeith, died in Tacna, Peru, on 21 December 1873. [S#9659]

BARRY, MARGARET, widow of John Bethune of Lumlair, Berbice, died in Forres on 4 August 1837. [AJ#4676]

BASCOM, JAMES ALEXANDER, husband of Louise Younger, niece and adopted daughter of Mrs Munro, Viewfield House, Merchiston, Midlothian, died at La Grange, Demerara, in 1883. [S#12,549]

BATCHELOR, GEORGE ANDREW, in Lima, married Catalina Maria Guerin from New York, in Lima on 9 August 1878. [EC#29297]

BAXTER, ARNOTT, born 1844, an engineer from Burntisland, Fife, died in Callao on 21 March 1873. [S#9306]

BAXTER, JAMES, eldest son of Arnot Baxter, Burntisland, died in Callao, Peru, on 30 April 1885. [S#13402]

BAYLEY, ..., son of Francis Walter Bayley, was born in Chorrilles, Peru, on 18 September 1878. [EC#29358]

BAYNE, ROBERT, in Buenos Ayres, son of Reverend Charles John Bayne and Jane Duguid in Fodderty, Aberdeenshire, around 1853. [NAS.S/H]

BEATSON, W. D., late in Edinburgh, youngest son of John Beatson in Kirkcaldy, died in Georgetown, Demerara, on 29 July 1837. [FH]

BEATTIE, MAXWELL, born 1804, a servant, emigrated from Leith to Buenos Ayres on the Symmetry, master William Cochrane, on 22 May 1825, landed there on 11 August 1825. [SRP#18]

BEATTON, JOHN WILLIAM, a clerk, son of John Beatton in Stromness, Orkney, died at Rio Grande do Sol, Brazil, on 1 November 1878. [EC#29393]; cnf 1879 Edinburgh. [NAS.SC70.1.195/1]

BEAVIS, JOHN, a plumber from Edinburgh, died in Mexico on 20 June 1867. [S#7512]

BECK, EDWARD, died in Rio de Janeiro, cnf Edinburgh 1891. [NAS.SC70.1.335/514]

BEGG, DAVID, from Musselburgh, East Lothian, emigrated to Poyais, died in Belize during 1823. [EEC#17520]

BEGG, WILLIAM, born in 1802, son of George Begg (1764-1856) a farmer, and Jane Walker (1764-1834), died in Guatamala during 1826. [Glentanar g/s]

BEGLIE, ALEXANDER, a surgeon in Surinam, 9 August 1831. [NAS.RS.Edinburgh.38/174]

BELL, JOHN, minister of All Saints Presbyterian Church, Berbice, 1843-1850. [F.7.673]

BELL, JOHN CHARLES, M.D., eldest son of R. C. Bell, M.D., Chile and Dumfriesshire, died in Copipo, Chile, on 3 August 1878. [S#10,979]

BELL, ELLEN, wife of Lauchlan Campbell McGoun a merchant in Guanaxuato, Mexico, died there 4 January 1869. [MAGU#12869][S#7969][ANY.2.229]

BELL, GEORGE, sometime a merchant in London, died in Acoyapa, Central America, on 20 October 1841. Cnf 1849 Edinburgh

BELL, GEORGE M., married Maggie Robson, in Quilmes, Buenos Ayres, on 9 July 1868. [S#7817]

BELL, JAMES, youngest son of John Bell in Lanark, died in Ascuncion del Paraguay on 9 April 1870. [S#8347]

BELL, JAMES, born 1852, died in Buenos Ayres in 1871. [SRP#365]

BELL, JANE MARGARET, only daughter of Thomas Bell married Albertus Thierens of Plantation Wisselvagheid, in Leguan, Demerara, on 18 October 1839. [SG#8/833]

BELL, JOHN EDWARD, second son of James Bell, SSC, North Bridge, Edinburgh, was killed at Tucuman, Argentina, on 1 December 1876. [S#10,420]

BELL, ROBERT, son of John Bell in Glasgow, died in Demerara during October 1819. [EA#5847/375]

BELL, Dr ROBERT CARLYLE, MD, born in 1816, from Newhall, Lockerbie, Dumfries-shire, died in Copiapo, Chile, on 9 June 1875. [EC#28340][AO]; cnf 1876 Edinburgh. [NAS.SC70.1.177/314]

BELL, THOMAS, born 1798, a bailliff, emigrated from Leith to Buenos Ayres on the Symmetry, master William Cochrane, on 22 May 1825, landed there on 11 August 1825. [SRP#18]

BELL, THOMAS, son of Peter Bell a smith at Pitcox, East lothian, died in Buenos Ayres on 18 May 1863. [S#2516]

BENNETT, D., from Kirkcaldy, married Elizabeth, daughter of W. Jex, in Belize, British Honduras, on 19 October 1869. [FA]

BENNET, JOHN ROSE, in Demerara, died 26 march 1821, cnf 1827 Edinburgh.

BERRY, ..., daughter of James Berry from Kirkcaldy, born on 5 March 1861 in San Jose, Costa Rica. [FH]

BERRY, MARIE, eldest daughter of James Berry from Kirkcaldy, married Don Mateo Mara, a merchant and coffee planter, in San Jose on 7 June 1866. [FH]

BERRY, MOSES, born 1803, a carpenter, emigrated from Leith to Buenos Ayres on the Symmetry, master William Cochrane, on 22 May 1825, landed there on 11 August 1825. [SRP#19]

BERTIE, JAMES, eldest son of James Bertie, Brechin and Edinburgh, married Victorina Carrera, only daughter of James Carrera in Gibralter, in Rosario de Santa Fe, South America, on 24 October 1879. [S#11,371]

BEST, MARY, born 1825, wife of Thomas Owler, late of Newport, Fife, died in Chascomus, Buenos Ayres, on 3 May 1891. [PJ]

BETHUNE, HUGH, youngest son of Reverend John Bethune in Alness, Ross and Cromarty, died in Berbice on 18 October 1821. [AJ#3861]

BETHUNE, JOHN, second son of Reverend John Bethune in Dornoch, Ross and Cromarty, died in Berbice during August 1804. [SM#66/885]

BETHUNE, JOHN, born in Alness on 2 October 1774, son of Reverend Angus Bethune and Catherine Munro, settled in Berbice, died on 18 April 1819. [F.7.27]

BEVERIDGE, ANDREW, born 1789, son of Michael Beveridge the Customs Controller of Kirkcaldy, Fife, died in Demerara on 17 November 1819. [S#4/169]

BEVERIDGE, HENRY, born 1798, son of Michael Beveridge the Customs Controller of Kirkcaldy, Fife, died in Demerara on 17 November 1819. [BM#7/231][S#4/169]

BEVERIDGE, JOHN, born 1846, third son of Reverend J.G.Beveridge in Inveresk, Midlothian, was killed by Indians near Bahia Blanca, South America, on 23 October 1870. [S#8647]

BIRCH, JOHN FORBES, died in Mexico, cnf 1884 Edinburgh. [NAS.SC70.1.232/261]

BIRSS, ROBERT, jr., born in 1857, second son of Robert Birss a wholesale druggist in Aberdeen, died in Georgetown, Demerara, on 3 June 1884. [AJ: 9.6.1884]

BISSET, JOHN LAW, from Brechin, Angus, then a merchant in Rio de Janeiro, cnf Edinburgh 1900. [NAS.SC70.1.396/516]

BISSET, THOMAS, in Guina during 1815. [NAS.SC.Perth: 10/177]

BLACK, ADAM FERGUS, in Essequibo, cnf 1874 Edinburgh. [NAS.SC70.1.167/443]

BLACK or FAIR, CHRISTINA, from Edinburgh, died at Sao Pedro, Punuis River, Brazil,cnf 1884 Edinburgh. [NAS.SC70.1.229/445]

BLACK, Mrs ELIZABETH, wife of James Black, died in Buenos Ayres on 17 May 1860. [DC#23516][S#1574]

BLACK, JAMES TAYLOR, born 1850, son of Robert Black and Isabella Dow, died in Valparaiso on 16 October 1894. [Ferry Port on Craig g/s, Fife]

BLACK, JAMES, son of George Black in Sorbie, Wigtonshire, a merchant in Monte Video, died on 17 December 1818. [S#118/19]

BLACK, JAMES, born 1796 in Woodhead, Buittle, Kirkcudbrightshire, died in Calle Temple, Buenos Ayres, on 31 October 1874. [S#9796]

BLACK, JOHN, an engineer from Kirkcaldy, married Eliza, daughter of Robert Brand in Kirkcaldy, in Rio de Janeiro on 31 August 1875, parents of sons born in Campos, Rio de Janeiro, on 6 August 1876 and on 13 January 1878.[FH]; in Campos, Rio de Janeiro, 1883. [NAS.RS.Kirkcaldy.20.196]

BLACK, ..., son of James Black an engineer from Kirkcaldy, Fife, was born in Campos, Rio de Janeiro, on 13 January 1878. [EC#29137][S#10,787]

BLACK, ..., son of John Black an engineer from Kirkcaldy, Fife, was born in Campos, Rio de Janeiro, on 24 November 1880. [S#11,376]

BLACKIE, BURRIDGE PURVIS, died in Cuba during 1851, cnf 1865 Edinburgh. [NAS.SC70.1.124/292]

BLACKIE, JAMES HAMILTON, son of Alexander Blackie a banker in Aberdeen, died off the coast of Chile in 1851. [AJ#5398][W#1232]

BLAIR, ALEXANDER, a sheepfarmer in Buenos Ayres, cnf 1871 Edinburgh. [NAS.SC70.1.154/22]

BLAIN, JAMES, probably from Greenock, Renfrewshire, a merchant in San Domingo, by 1839. [NAS.SH.22.11.1839]

BLAIR, JOHN, born 25 February 1741, in Brechin, Angus, son of Reverend David Blair and Christian Doig, settled in Providence, Essequibo. [F.5.376]

BLAIR, JOHN, married Amy Landsborough, in Valparaiso on 1 April 1874. [S#9629]

BLAIR, GEORGE, son of Thomas Blair a farmer in Hoprig Mains, East Lothian, married Margaret Drysdale, daughter of R. P. Drysdale the Mayor of Georgetown, and widow of Rev. J. E.Gummer, in Georgetown, Demerara, on 10 August 1881. [S#11,909]

BLAIR, THOMAS OGILVY MCQUATER, born 1831, son of James Blair [1796-1833] and Mary McQuater [1791-1863], died in Tampico 21 July 1852. [New Dailly g/s, Ayrshire]

BLAIR, WILLIAM, an engine driver in Maestranzadel, Valparaiso, Chile, by 1890, son of William Blair, a baker in Bathgate, West Lothian. [NAS.SH.22.2.1890]

BLAIR, ..., son of George Blair a merchant, was born in Georgetown, Demerara, on 17 February 1878. [S#11,139]

BLAKE, THOMAS, son of William Blake and Agnes Mowat, a merchant in Mexico, 1534-1585. [AUL]

BLYTH, THOMAS, born 1852, a boilermaker from Leven, Fife, died in Callao on 31 May 1889. [People's Journal]

BONE, HELEN, born 1800, a servant, emigrated from Leith to Buenos Ayres on the Symmetry, master William Cochrane, on 22 May 1825, landed there on 11 August 1825. [SRP#19]

BOOG, Captain MACDUFF HART, married Eliza, daughter of Mr Thornton of Cummingsburg, in Demerara on 10 January 1820. [BM#7.231]

BOOG, WILLIAM, born 1 December 1783, a merchant in Rio de Janeiro. [F.3.166]

BORLAND, FRANCIS, born 1666, son of John Borland in East Kilbride, educated at Glasgow University, emigrated before 1685, a minister in Surinam, died in Lanarkshire during 1722. [F#7/662][HMC.Laing#I.331; EUL.Laing\III.262]

BORMAN, OLIVIA M. L., in Georgetown, Demerara, 4 September 1879. [NAS.SC70.6]

BORROWMAN, THOMSON, born in 1824, son of Robert Borrowman and Elizabeth Stevenson, died at the Caledonian Foundry, Valparaiso, on 26 August 1876. [Greyfriars g/s, Edinburgh] [S#10,374]

BOTER, JAMES, from Demerara, educated at King's College, Aberdeen, from 1818 to 1822. [AUL]

BOUSIE, JOHN, late tenant of Kirkton Barns, Forgan, Fife, was murdered at the Mines of Arroa, Columbia, on 8 August 1836. [FH, 3.11.1836]

BOWAN, DAVID WILLIAM, born 1817, an engineer in Pernambuco, died in Broughty Ferry on 1 March 1872. [Monifieth g/s, Angus]

BOWEN, JAMES, in Lebu, Chile, cnf 1878 Edinburgh. [NAS.SC70.1.189/430]

BOWER, JOHN, born in 1821, son of Alexander and Helen Bower, a shipmaster who died in Panama on 22 April 1853. [St Andrews g/s, Fife]

BOWHILL, JOHN, son of Thomas Bowhill in Ayton, Berwickshire, married Amelia Ejarabido, in Passo de los Torros, Costa del Rio Negra, Uruguay, on 20 September 1882. [S#12,299]

BOWIE, HENRY SCRUTTON, only son of Alexander Bowie in Paisley, Renfrewshire, died in Demerara on 13 July 1846. [EEC#21389][NAS.CC8.8.inv.1848]

BOWIE, or SCOTT, MARION R., in Valparaiso, 1880. [NAS.RS. Paisley.6.143]

BOWMAN, LIZZIE, second daughter of David William Bowman of Pernambuco and Broughty Ferry, married John Robert, in London 30 August 1870. [S#8454]

BOYD, ..., daughter of John Pringle Boyd, was born in Buenos Ayres on 2 February 1867. [S#7377]

BOYD, ROBERT, born 1804, a servant, emigrated from Leith to Buenos Ayres on the Symmetry, master William Cochrane, on 22 May 1825, landed there on 11 August 1825. [SRP#19]

BOYD, WILLIAM, born 1781, youngest son of Thomas Boyd of Kilmarnock, Jamaica, died in Demerara during 1804. [AJ#2652]

BOYD, ..., son of John P. Boyd, was born in Buenos Ayres on 15 July 1863. [S#2567]

BOYLE, CATHERINE, wife of William Paterson a plumber, from Edinburgh, died in Mexico on 24 December 1876. [S#10,464]

BRAID, THOMAS, second son of Alexander Braid an innkeeper in Renfrew, died in Berbice on 14 January 1842. [GSP#707]

BRANDER, ALEXANDER, in Buenos Ayres before 1856. [NAS.S/H]

BRASH, WILLIAM BAIN, born in 1824, died in Moron, Buenos Ayres on 15 April 1878. [EC#29233]; cnf 1870 Edinburgh. [NAS.SC70.1.146/579]

BRAUD, ..., daughter of Arthur Braud, was born at Pin Mon Repos, Demerara, on 1 December 1875. [EC#28472]

BRAUD, ..., daughter of Arthur Braud, was born at Plantation Mon Repos, Demerara, on 24 November 1878. [EC#29412]

BREMNER, ALEXANDER, born in 1793 son of James Bremner, a farmer, and Isobel Ord, died in Demerara on 14 February 1820. [Speymouth-Dipple g/s]

BREMNER, JOHN, son of James Bremner late in Kirkcaldy, Fife, died in Lima, Peru, on 11 March 1889. [FFP]

BREMNER, ..., son of James Bremner, late of Linktown, Kirkcaldy, manager of the Chorollos Gas Works in Peru, born 27 March 1871. [FA][S#8674]

BRIDGES, JAMES, sixth son of Francis Bridges in Edinburgh, died in Berbice on 9 September 1846. [EEC#21413]

BRIDGES, PETER, son of Francis Bridges in Edinburgh, late of Demerara, died in New South Wales, on 18 December 1877. [EC#29134]

BRIGGS, CHARLES SELKRIG, born 1811, youngest son of Alexander Briggs a wine-merchant in Dalkeith, Midlothian, died in Demerara on 18 January 1832. [EEC#18775][GkAd#3824]

BRIGGS, DAVID, merchant in Rio de Janeiro, 1817, son of John Briggs and his wife Mary Reston in Kirkcaldy, Fife. [NAS.SH.28.4.1817]

BRIGGS, JANE, youngest daughter of George Briggs a grate and stone manufacturer in Haddington, East Lothian, married John Wright, in Rio de Janeiro on 10 September 1873. [S#9435]

BRITTAIN, ..., son of George A. Brittain, was born in Buenos Ayres on 22 December 1861. [S#1761]

BROACH, JAMES, born 1801, a farmer, with his sister, emigrated from Leith to Buenos Ayres on the Symmetry, master William Cochrane, on 22 May 1825, landed there on 11 August 1825. [SRP#19]

BROADFOOT, WALLACE, second son of John Broadfoot a merchant in Leith, stepson of Reverend R. W. Thomson in Kirn, died on Zeelght Plantation, Demerara, 5 January 1871, [S#8583]; a planter in Demerara, cnf 1871 Edinburgh. [NAS.SC70.1.154/707]

BRODIE, ALEXANDER, son of William Brodie of Endrick Bank, died off Monte Video, River Plate, on 11 February 1839. [SG#8/770]

BRODIE, DAVID, born in 1819, son of James Brodie a merchant in Glasgow, died in Demerara on 23 May 1838. [SG#7/681]

BRODIE, JOHN P., son of William Brodie [1780-1846] a schoolmaster in Alloa, Clackmannanshire, settled in Mexico. [Alloa g/s]

BRODIE, JOHN, Plantation, Richmond Hill, British Guiana, died 12 May 1840, inventory, 1840 Edinburgh.

BROWN, Dr ALEXANDER, born 1819, son of David Brown, Roseland Cottage, Linlithgow, West Lothian, died in Chillan, Chile, on 30 October 1874. [S#9796]

BROWN, Reverend ARCHIBALD, born in Paisley, Renfrewshire, during 1787, son of Robert Brown a farmer, educated at the University of Edinburgh, a minister in Demerara from 1818 to 1824, died in Edinburgh on 8 November 1843. [F#7/674]; in Demerara on 11 September 1826, [NAS.RD#322/626]; and on 28 January 1829, [NAS.RD#379/414][cnf Edinburgh 1844]

BROWN, DAVID, eldest son of ...... Brown a surveyor in Kelso, Roxburghshire, died in Chillean, Chile, 26 July 1869. [S#8164]

BROWN, Dr GORDON, born on 2 July 1784, son of Reverend Brown and Isabella Ord in New Spynie, educated at Marischal College, Aberdeen, from 1799 to 1802, a physician in Demerara, father of Ann, died in Demerara on 16 July 1813. [NAS.PS3.15.149] [F#6/407][EA#5192/13][AJ#3430] [MCA]

BROWN, JAMES, born 1800, a servant, with his wife Mary and one child, emigrated from Leith to Buenos Ayres on the Symmetry on 22 May 1825, landed there on 11 August 1825. [SRP#19]

BROWN, JAMES, born 1799, a servant, emigrated from Leith to Buenos Ayres on the Symmetry on 22 May 1825, landed there on 11 August 1825. [SRP#19]

BROWN, JAMES, a gardener from Edinburgh, emigrated to Poyais, died in Belize during 1823. [EEC#17520]

BROWN, JAMES, a merchant in Buenos Ayres, married Mary Christina Latham, eldest daughter of Wilfred Latham of Buenos Ayres, at Maldonedo, Rio de la Plata, on 9 April 1863. [S#2452]

BROWN, JAMES PENNYCOOK, Fellow of the Royal Geographical Society, from Elgin, Morayshire, died at Sierra de Cocaes, Minas Gercies, Brazil, on 11 February 1873.[EC#27613]

BROWN, JANET, born 1799, a servant, emigrated from Leith to Buenos Ayres on the Symmetry on 22 May 1825, landed there on 11 August 1825. [SRP#19]

BROWN, MARGARET, daughter of James Brown a surgeon in Saltcoats, Ayrshire, wife of Robert Alison, died in Bellavista, Callao, on 8 March 1873. [S#9287]

BROWN, THOMAS, a merchant in Mexico, married Joanna, eldest daughter of John Gibson, a plumber in Leith, at Trinity Villa on 5 July 1831. [PA#101]

BROWN, WILLIAM, a Presbyterian minister in Buenos Ayres from 1826 to 1850. [F#7/681][NLS#3437/251]

BROWN, WILLIAM, born 1840, chief engineer of the Chilean Navy, died in Valparaiso on 2 May 1877. [S#10,554]

BROWN, ..., son of Archibald Galbraith Brown, was born in Pernambuco, Brazil, on 11 October 1883. [S#12,579]

BRUCE, LAURENCE B., born 1836, died in Mexico on 21 September 1904. [Cargill g/s, Perthshire]

BRUCE, ROBERT, second son of James Bruce, a farmer in Colluthie, Gartly, died in Laraquete, Chile, on 6 September 1887. [AJ:14.11.1887]

BRUCE, WILLIAM, born in 1850, brother of George Bruce, a cycle agent in Aberdeen, died in Guadaloupe, Peru, on 24 July 1898. [AJ:16.9.1898]

BRYCE, ANN, born 1841, died in Buenos Ayres in 1871. [SRP#365]

BRYMNER, ALEXANDER, jr., late of Greenock, died in Belize, Honduras, on 5 August 1839. [SG#8/804]

BRYSON, PETER, from Leith, married Mary Smith, second daughter of James Smith in Kinleith, Currie, Midlothian, in Valparaiso on 28 September 1869. [S#8206]

BRYSON, ROBERT, married Jane McGill Maxton, daughter of Peter Maxton, a shipowner in Greenock, in Lima on 21 February 1876. [EC#28552][S#10,203]

BRYSON, ..., daughter of John B. Bryson, was born in Lima, Peru, on 1 February 1878. [EC#29184]

BRYSON, ..., daughter of Peter Bryson from Leith, was born in Valparaiso on 3 October 1871. [S#8842]

BRYSON, ..., son of Peter Bryson from Leith, was born in La
Cabriterra, Valparaiso on 16 February 1873. [S#9308]

BUCHAN-HEPBURN, JOHN GEORGE, born 24 September 1841,
eldest son of Sir Thomas Buchan-Hepburn of Smeaton-
Hepburn, died on 21 January 1883 in Pinos Altos, Chihuahua,
Mexico. [Prestonkirk g/s]

BUCHANAN, General ALEXANDER, died in Surinam during
November 1801, cnf 22 September 1807 Edinburgh

BUCHANAN, Reverend ANDREW, minister of the Scots Church in
the parish of St Clement's, Berbice, died at the house of Miss
Mary Orr in Charlestown, Berbice, on 28 September 1839.
[EEC#19982][SG#8/825][Doune g/s, Perthshire] [F.7.676]

BUCHANAN, GEORGE, born 1830, eldest son John Buchanan in
Finnich, Drymen, Stirlingshire, an insurance agent in
Valparaiso, died in Limache, Chile, on 18 November 1880, cnf
Edinburgh 1888. [NAS.SC70.1.267/398][S#11,700]

BUCHANAN, HUGH, son of Reverend Dr Buchanan in Glasgow,
died in Georgetown, Demerara, 1852. [S.23.10.1852]

BUCHANAN, JOHN, son of the late John Cross Buchanan,
Auchintoshan, Dunbarton, married Rosa Henrietta Jenken,
second daughter of late Thomas Jenken, MD, of Zacatecas,
Mexico, in the British Consulate there on 4 March 1865.
[GM.NS2/18.778]

BUCHANAN of AUCHMAR, JOHN, jr., died in Georgetown,
Demerara on 20 July 1823. [BM#14/624][EEC#17512]

BUCHANAN, JOHN, jr., in Valparaiso, cnf Edinburgh 1888.
[NAS.SC70.1.267/393]

BUCHANAN, JOHN HENRY, born 1875, only son of John
Buchanan of Valparaiso, died there on 16 December 1898.
[S#17343]

BUCHANAN, ROBERT, a sheep farmer in Buenos Ayres, son of
Helen Wright or Buchanan or MacKean who died 6 May 1875.
[NAS.12.11.1896]

BUDGE, ROBERT FORBES, a merchant in Valparaiso, later a
surgeon in Lerwick, Shetland Islands, 20 December 1841.
[NAS.RGS#225/29]

BUIK, ROBERT, born in 1809, son of Robert Buik [1783-1832] and Jean Dick, died in St Louis, South America, on 28 October 1832. [Aberdour g/s, Fife]

BUIST, DAVID, born 1848, son of Mathew Buist in Tynningham, died in South America on 6 February 1883. [S#12,331]

BUIST, GEORGE, born 1780, a carpenter in Cupar, Fife, indentured to serve Lieutenant Colonel George Bell, 39th Regiment of Foot, and Wolf Katz, in their plantation of Bachelors' Adventure in Berbice for three years, subscribed on 25 March 1801. [NAS.SC20.33.14]

BUIST, GEORGE WILLIAM MASSON, born 1831, from St Andrews, Fife, an engineer in Itapebi, Salto Banda Oriental, died there on 10 May 1880, cnf 1881 Edinburgh. [S#11,530] [NAS.SC70.1.205/183]

BUIST, WILLIAM, son of William Buist in Kilconquhar Mill, Fife, died in Para, Brazil, on 17 April 1879. [EFR]

BURGESS, JAMES, son of William Burgess in Rothes, Morayshire, who died in November 1831, settled in Demerara and Essequibo. [NAS.SH.1867]

BURGESS, THOMAS, a boatbuilder in Slateford, Midlothian, emigrated to Poyais, died 1823. [EEC#17520]

BURN, WILLIAM, son of George Burn in Glasgow, died in Demerara on 12 January 1842. [GSP#707]

BURNETT, ARCHIBALD, born in 1835, son of John Burnett a writer in Glasgow, matriculated at Glasgow University in 1849, died in Monte Video on 5 September 1869. [MAGU

BURNETT, JAMES, an attorney at law, eldest son of James Burnett of Barns, died in Georgetown, Demerara, on 6 December 1836. [AJ#4647][Manor g/s, Peebles-shire]

BURNETT, JOHN E., a merchant in Demerara, a deed witness. [NAS.RD3.295.657]

BURNS, ROBERT, born 1797, a trainer, with his wife Anne and one child, emigrated from Leith to Buenos Ayres on the Symmetry on 22 May 1825, landed there on 11 August 1825. [SRP#19]

BURNS, WILLIAM, born 1794, a servant, with his wife Elizabeth and two children, emigrated from Leith to Buenos Ayres on the Symmetry on 22 May 1825, landed there on 11 August 1825. [SRP#19]

BUTCHART, ALEXANDER, with his wife and their children George born 1815, Caroline born 1820, and Alexander born 1825, emigrated from Cromarty on the Planet of London, Captain William Barclay, on 1 October 1825, landed at La Guayra on 2 December 1825, settled at Topo, Columbia, by 1827. [PRO.FO.18/47; FO.199/3/32]

BUTCHART, PETER, with his wife and their children Jane born 1812, Ann born 1814, Jesse born 1815, David born 1824, and Edward Stopford born 1826, emigrated from Cromarty on the Planet of London, Captain William Barclay, on 1 October 1825, landed at La Guayra on 2 December 1825, settled at Topo, Columbia, by 1827. [PRO.FO.18/47; FO.199/3/32]

BUTCHART, ROBERT, with his wife and their children Sarah born 1817, Ann born 1814, James born 1820, and Helen born 1826, emigrated from Cromarty on the Planet of London, Captain William Barclay, on 1 October 1825, landed at La Guayra on 2 December 1825, settled at Topo, Columbia, by 1827. [PRO.FO.18/47; FO.199/3/32]

BUTLER, Mrs, wife of Joseph Butler, a merchant in Dumfries, died in Carthagena on 30 September 1808. [SM#70/959]

BUTTERS, ADAM, settled on the River Plate, Argentina, in 1822. [SRP#21]

CAIRNS, JOHN, jr., youngest son of John Cairns, station agent at Ponfeigh, Lanark, died 16 February 1871 on the brig Eliada of London, at Waterloo Estate, Nickerie, Surinam. [S#8623]

CALDER, ADAM, elder son of Adam Calder in Belhaven, East Lothian, died in Pergamino, South America, in 1879. [S#11,410]

CALDER, ALEXANDER GORDON, youngest child of William Calder, died at Plantation friends, Berbice, British Guiana, on 4 December 1873. [S#9499]

CALDER, Mrs MARY ELIZABETH, born 1850, wife of William M. Calder, died in Stewartville, West Coast, Demerara, on 24 February 1877. [S#10,514]

CALDER, WILLIAM, youngest son of Alexander Calder in Edinburgh, married Mary Elizabeth Williams, daughter of Mr Williams in Berbice, there on 15 April 1869. [S#8063]

CALLANDER, RANDAL, HM Consul, second son of R. W. M.

Callander jr of Craigforth, died at Rio Grande du Sol on 3 June 1877. [EC#28951]

CALLANDER, ROBERT, of the London and River Plate Bank, married Angela Emma Manuela Milbourne, in Monte Video on 17 October 1868. [S#7909]

CALLANDER, ROBERT, eldest son of Robert Callander in Falkirk, died in Colonia, South America, on 20 November 1884. [S#12955]

CALLUM, JOHN REID, born 1844, eldest son of John Callum a merchant in Edinburgh, died in Georgetown, Demerara, on 29 October 1862. [S#2329]

CAMERON, DONALD CHARLES, in Berbice, husband of Elizabeth Fraser Matheson, third daughter of Colin Matheson of Bennetsfield, 1817. [NAS.RD5.126.385]; a merchant in Berbice 1816-1833, [NAS.CS96.972]

CAMERON, EDWARD STEWART, born in 1779, Commissioner and Secretary in South America of the Chilean Mining Association, died on 19 June 1833. [SG#2/154]

CAMERON, GEORGE, born in Dundee son of James Cameron, a merchant, and Margaret Walker, died in Mexico during 1867. [Dundee, Constitution Road, g/s]

CAMERON, JAMES, born 1808, son of Alexander Cameron and Mary Davidson, died in Demerara on 10 June 1840. [Little Dunkeld g/s, Perthshire]

CAMERON, JANE, eldest daughter of David Cameron an iron-founder in Bahia, Brazil, married Alexander Smith an engineer from Aberdeen, at HM Consulate in Bahia on 5 December 1863. [AJ#6053]

CAMERON, JOHN, a merchant in Berbice, 1817, 1820. [NAS.RD5.124.257; RD5.191.483]

CAMERON, JOHN, eldest son of Colin Cameron clerk of works at the Glasgow military depot, died in Demerara on 22 April 1833. [SG#150]

CAMERON, JOHN, of Glenevis, then in Berbice, 1850. [NAS.RS38.PR54/276]

CAMERON, JOHN, in New Amsterdam, South America, cnf 1859. [NAS.SC70.1.100/516]

CAMERON of BARCALDINE, JOHN, born on 27 June 1824, died in Berbice on 29 January 1857. [St Modans, Ardchattan, g/s]

CAMERON, JOHN, late in Berbice, then in Glenevis, 1848. [NAS.RS.Inverness#291]

CAMERON, LEWIS, in Demerara 1810. [NAS.GD23.10.667]

CAMERON, W., born 1847, died in Buenos Ayres in 1871. [SRP#365]

CAMPBELL, AGNES, born 1797, died in Buenos Ayres in 1871. [SRP#365]

CAMPBELL, ALEXANDER, St Catherine's, died in Demerara 1810. [EEC]

CAMPBELL, ANGUS, and his wife, emigrated from Cromarty on the Planet of London, Captain William Barclay, on 1 October 1825, landed at La Guayra on 2 December 1825, settled at Topo, Columbia, by 1827. [PRO.FO.18/47; FO.199/3/32]

CAMPBELL, ARCHIBALD JAMES, in La Chacra, Buenos Ayres, grandson of William Campbell a Writer to the Signet in Edinburgh who died 28 April 1849. [NAS.SH.30.1.1896]

CAMPBELL, CHRISTINA, daughter of D. Campbell in Leith, married Simon Kerr of the English Academy in Coquimba, South America, there on 30 March 1861. [S#1842]

CAMPBELL, COLIN, son of Mungo Campbell of Kinloch, in Brazil during 1728. [NAS.GD170/3076]

CAMPBELL, COLIN, in Demerara, married Mary Rose, eldest daughter of James Rose, Deputy Clerk of Session, in Edinburgh on 10 July 1821, [EA#6032/183]; Colin Campbell of Good Success, Essequibo, died in Georgetown, Demerara, on 29 September 1822. [SM#91/128][DPCA#1066]

CAMPBELL, DUGALD WILLIAM, born in Glassary, Argyll, on 6 June 1779, son of Reverend Peter Campbell and Margaret Scott, a merchant, died in Bahia on 11 August 1823. [BM#14/624][F.4.7]

CAMPBELL, DUNCAN, son of Duncan Neil Campbell of Knap, died in Demerara in August 1826. [BM#21/373][AJ#4124]

CAMPBELL, DUNCAN, Rosario de Santa Fe, late of Killin, Perthshire, married Catherine, youngest daughter of Rob Roy McGregor, Foss, Perthshire, at 334 Calle St Martin, Buenos Ayres, in 1868. [S#7872]

CAMPBELL, ELLEN, born 1846, died in Buenos Ayres in 1871. [SRP#365]

CAMPBELL, FREDERICK, born 1804, son of Lieutenant Donald Campbell of Fernicarry, Dunbartonshire, died at Estancia Macitas, province of Entre Rios, in 1868. [S#7675]

CAMPBELL, GEORGE WILLIAM, married margaret Collins, second daughter of John Collins, Santa Barbara, Gualequaychia, Entre Rios, there on 30 November 1871. [S#8898]

CAMPBELL, JOHN, of the Commissary Department, son of Patrick Campbell of the Royal Bank of Scotland in Edinburgh, died in Berbice on 10 December 1805. [SM#68/78][EEC#1806][AJ#3044]

CAMPBELL, JOHN, died in Scravendale, Holland, on arrival from Surinam on 21 November 1824. [SM#16/127]

CAMPBELL, JOHN, third son of John Campbell in Glasgow, married Mary Rosary Robson, second daughter of Peter Robson, Santa Elena, Entre Rios, in St Andrews, Buenos Ayres, on 24 February 1873. [EC#27877]

CAMPBELL, MARY ANN RAMSAY, wife of William Ranken, died at Golden Grove, Demerara, on 11 July 1846. [EEC#21388]

CAMPBELL, MARY ANNE, born 1843, died in Buenos Ayres in 1871. [SRP#365]

CAMPBELL, PATRICK, in Estancia Salado, Buenos Ayres, brother of George Campbell in Newton Stewart who died 9 May 1886. [NAS.SH.5.11.1888]

CAMPBELL, ROBERT, born in 1861, grandson of Mrs Blakie, East Bank Road, Aberdeen, died in Schoon Ord Estate, West Bank, Demerara, on 24 December 1861. [AJ:17.1.1882]

CAMPBELL, STEWART DUNCAN, settled on the River Plate, Argentina, in 1820. [SRP#20]; son of John Campbell, Clerk to the Signet, a merchant in Paraigo, Buenos Ayres, died on 16 June 1827. [BM#22/768]

CAMPBELL, THOMAS, of Grenada, died in Demerara on 14 May 1795. [EEC: 23.7.1795]

CAMPBELL, WILLIAM, in Collow, Valparaiso, 1881. [NAS.SC70.1.205/144]

CARGILL. JAMES, of the Venue Office, died in Cummingberg, Georgetown, Demerara, on 20 October 1841. [EEC#20302]

CARLYLE, JOHN, son of Captain John Carlyle, died in Rio de Janeiro on 16 May 1850. [Annan g/s, Dumfries-shire]

CARMICHAEL, H. L., Major General and Acting Governor, died in Demerara in 1813. [EA#5175/73]

CARRICK, ..., son of Robert Carrick, was born in Monte Video on 3 April 1871. [S#8681]

CARRUTHERS, JOHN J., from Annan, Dumfries-shire, died in Rio de Janeiro on 25 December 1893. [AO:4.5.1894]

CARRUTHERS, MARGARET, daughter of Reverend William Carruthers of South Queensferry, wife of Capitao Tenente Jose Maria Da Conceicao, died in Rio de Janeiro on 11 October 1877. [S#10,710]

CARSE, JAMES, in Demerara, died 18 February 1844. Cnf Edinburgh 1844

CARSTAIRS, GEORGE STEWART, of Potosi, born 1810, late a merchant in Leith, died at Plantation Caledonia, Surinam, on 7 June 1842. [EEC#20408]

CARSTAIRS, W. A., a Member of the Supreme Court, died in Surinam on 1 November 1821. [BM#40/263][EEC#17255][S#261]

CARTER, JOHN, a proprietor, settled on the River Plate, Argentina, in 1806. [SRP#20]

CATHCART, FREDERICK, Lieutenant Colonel, late HM Minister Plenipotentiary to the Germanic Confederation, Knight of the Thistle, married Jean McAdam of Craigengillan, in Berbice on 18 October 1827. [EEC#18113]

CATHCART, JAMES, born 1802, a surveyor, emigrated from Leith to Buenos Ayres on the Symmetry on 22 May 1825, landed there on 11 August 1825. [SRP#19]

CATTENACH, ALEXANDER KINNEAR, born 1811, son of Adam Cattenach in Fernieside, died in Tampico, Mexico, on 18 August 1843. [EEC#20667]

CAULFIELD, ..., daughter of Lieutenant James E. W. S. Caulfield of the 2nd West India Regiment, was born at Eve Leary Barracks, Georgetown, Demerara, on 1July 1877. [S#10,597]

CAY, THOMAS, son of the late Thomas Cay an advocate in Edinburgh, died at Rosario, Sante Fe, Argentina, on 25 February 1868. [S#7690]; cnf 1871 Edinburgh. [NAS.SC70.1.153/39]

CHALMERS, ANDREW, in Monte Video, cnf 1856 Edinburgh [NAS.SC70.1.91/595]

CHALMERS, WATSON, born 1843, fourth son of Richard Chalmers, 6 Mackenzie Place, Edinburgh, died in Rio de Janeiro 14 April 1860. [S#1551]

CHALMERS, WILLIAM, born in 1778, son of John Chalmers and Elizabeth Hall, died on the Queen in Rio de Janeiro during 1800. [Anstruther Easter g/s]

CHAPMAN, THOMAS, born in 1836, a merchant in Monte Video, died in Barnton, West Lothian, on 19 January 1874. [Cramond g/s]; cnf 1874 Edinburgh. [NAS.SC70.1.1679/102]

CHARLES, ALEXANDER H., born in 1857, son of A. H. Charles and Jeanne Steel, died on the Isle de Naos, Panama Bay, on 6 September 1885. [Burntisland g/s]

CHESSELL, WILLIAM, born 1800, a carpenter, emigrated from Leith to Buenos Ayres on the Symmetry on 22 May 1825, landed there on 11 August 1825. [SRP#19]

CHEYNE, WILLIAM STIELL, MD, late of Mexico, eldest son of Stuart Cheyne a merchant in Edinburgh, died in New York on 10 December 1841. [GH#4067]

CHISHOLM, ALEXANDER, son of Provost William Chisholm of Inverness, died at Friendship Plantation, Demerara, on 16 July 1799. [GC#1190]

CHISHOLM, ALEXANDER, from Ross-shire, married Eliza Mills from Hampshire, in Georgetown, Demerara, on 5 September 1840. [AJ#3844]

CHRISTIE, CHARLES MAITLAND, third son of Charles Maitland Christie of Durie, Leven, Fife, died in Colonia Alexandra, Argentina, on 14 September 1875. [EC#28422]

CHRISTIE, HELEN GRINDLAY, daughter of Andrew Christie in Dunfermline, Fife, married Archibald M. McQueen, a merchant, in Valparaiso on 10 June 1865. [FA]

CHRISTIE, JOHN, born in 1833, son of George Christie and Christine Strobie, died in Rio de Janeiro on 7 February 1853. [Ferryport-on-Craig g/s, Fife]

CHRISTIE, ROBERT JOHN CRAIG, married Harriet Mary Dalzell, in Valparaiso, Chile, on 14 May 1881. [S#11,849]

CHRISTIE, ..., son of Robert John Craig Christie, was born in Valparaiso on 28 June 1882. [S#12,195]

CLARK, ANDREW LEES, of Assloss, born on 4 August 1835, son of James Clark, boot and shoe manufacturer, [1788-1871] and Margaret Reid [died in 1879], late of Rio de Janeiro, died on 2 April 1884. [Kilmarnock Laigh g/s, Ayrshire]

CLARK, DANIEL ALEXANDER, born 1818, chief engineer of the Peruvian Government Service, died in Callao, Peru, in 1871. [S#8891]

CLARK, DAVID, born 1858, eldest son of Andrew Clark, hallkeeper, Corn Exchange, Kirkcaldy, died in Georgetown, British Guina, on 6 April 1885. [PJ]

CLARK, GEORGE, of High Drumley, born on 17 April 1815, son of Thomas Clark [1784-1855] and Martha Anderson [1792-1838], late of Rio de Janeiro, died on 26 August 1874. [Kilmarnock Laigh g/s, Ayrshire]

CLARK, JAMES, of Blanefield, Kirkoswald, born on 14 September 1819, son of Thomas Clark [1784-1855] and Martha Anderson [1792-1838], late of Rio de Janeiro, died on 6 October 1879. [Kilmarnock Laigh g/s, Ayrshire]

CLARK, JOHN, planter in Demerara, died 1809. [NAS.CC8.8.138]

CLARK, MARY, youngest daughter of Robert Clark in Newburgh, Fife, married John Storrar manager of the Vryheids Lust Plantation, at Montrose House, East Coast, Demerara on 11 October 1876. [Fife Herald][S#10,397]

CLARK, THOMAS MCCRAN, born 1854, M.B., C.M., University of Edinburgh, died in Georgetown, Demerara, on 24 August 1878. [S#10,969]

CLARK, WILLIAM, a surgeon on Leyman Island, Essequibo, died 3 February 1839. Cnf 1852 Edinburgh [NAS.CC8.8.inv.1842]

CLUNIE, FRANCIS, son of John and Barbara Clunie in Lindores, Fife, died in Ancud, Chile, on 16 September 1897. [PJ]

COATS, Dr HENRY, in Rio de Janeiro, 1849.
[NAS.SC58.59.21.111]

COCHRANE, ALEXANDER, shipping agent and consul at
Mollendo and at Arequipas, Peru, from 1879 to 1883.
[NAS.RH2.8.94,1]

COCHRANE, GEORGE, of Robert Cochrane and Sons in Paisley,
died in Sansonate, Mexico, on 24 August 1824. [DPCA#1149]

COCHRANE, GEORGE, a merchant from Paisley, Renfrewshire,
then in South America, 1825. [NAS.RS54.2963]

COCHRANE, MATTHEW, merchant of the House of John Begg
and Company, in Lima, Peru, 1826-1828. [NAS.RH4.31.21]

COCHRANE, GEORGE, in Valparaiso, 1856. [NAS.SC58.59.24.45]

COCHRANE, Captain JOHN DUNDAS, died in Valencia,
Columbia, on 12 August 1825. [DPCA#1212]

COCHRANE, THOMAS, in Rio de Janeiro, 1823.
[NLS.ms591.1779]

COCHRANE, Sir THOMAS, 10th Earl of Dundonald, Commander in
Chief of the Chilean Navy and then of the Brazilian Navy,
1818-1860. [NAS.GD233]

COCKBURN, ..., daughter of S. A. Cockburn of Belize,
Honduras, was born at Cape Gracias a Dios on 18 November
1878. [EC#29449]

COGHILL, DONALD J. M., eldest son of Alexander Coghill agent
of the Commercial Bank of Scotland in Stromness, Orkney,
married Valentina Vila, eldest daughter of Luis Vila, in Monte
Video on 31 October 1882. [S#12,316]

COLEMAN, HENRY WILLIAM ALEXANDER, MD, married
Charlotte Sophie Martin, eldest daughter of Colonel Martin of
the 16th Lancers, in Valparaiso on 12 November 1859.
[DC#23468][S#1431]

COLLINGS, AUGUSTUS, born in 1841, second son of Stephen
Collings a merchant in Rio de Janeiro, on 28 February 1878.
[EC#29182]

COLLINS, Mrs HECTORINA, born in Inverness, wife of Mr Collins a
merchant in Georgetown, died on Plantation Amsterdam,
Demerara, on 25 February 1844. [AJ#5024]

COLLINS, THOMAS, minister in Valparaiso 1893. [F.7.684]

COLQUHOUN, ..., daughter of Alexander Colquhoun MD, of St John del Rey Mining Company, was born in Morro Velha, Rio de Janeiro, on 24 February 1878. [EC#29178]

COLT, ..., daughter of H. D. Colt, was born in Gualeguachu, Entre Rios, Argentina, on 8 August 1874. [EC#28100]

COLTART, Reverend ROBERT, born 1800, from Abbotshall, Kirkcaldy, educated at St Andrews University, minister of St Mark's, British Guiana, 1839-1840, died at the Manse of St Mark's, Demerara, on 22 June 1840. [AJ#4834][F.7.678]

COOKE, WILLIAM, born 1794, eldest son of William Cooke rector of Hamilton Grammar School, died in Augustura on the River Orinicco in 1820. [GkAd#2379]

CORBETT, CLEMENTINA GIBSON, infant daughter of George Corbett, died at Estancia los Inglesias, Ajo, Buenos Ayres, on 27 May 1884. [S#12875]

CORBETT, GEORGE, son of William Corbett, Melville Street, Portobello, Midlothian, married Helen Margaret McGregor, fourth daughter of J. W. McGregor in Glasgow, in Buenos Ayres 8 June 1871. [S#8725]

CORBETT, JOHN, a merchant in Demerara, 1801. [GA.T-ARD#13/1]

CORBETT,......., daughter of George Corbett was born at Estancia de los Inglesias, Tuyu, on 17 May 1872. [S#9041]

CORBETT,......., daughter of George Corbett was born at Estancia de los Inglesias, Buenos Ayres, on 10 January 1874. [S#9537]

CORBETT, ...,, son of George Corbett, was born at Estancia de los Ingleses, Buenos Ayres, on 2 April 1876. [S#10,209]

CORBETT, ..., son of George Corbett, was born at the Estancia de los Inglesias-Ajo, Buenos Ayres, on 9 January 1882. [S#12,045]

CORBETT, ..., daughter of George Corbett, was born at the Estancia de los Inglesias, Ajo, Buenos Ayres, on 4 November 1883. [S#12,615]

CORMACK, WILLIAM HINE, born 1843, purser of the Royal Mail Packet Company, eldest son of Sir John Rose Cormack, MD in Paris, died in Novo Friburgo, Brazil, on 8 April 1872. [S#8991]

CORNFOOT, ANDREW JAMES, born in Largo, Fife, during 1807, died in Burnside, Surinam, during 1830. [BM#28.574]

CORSTORPHINE, CHARLES, died in Georgetown, Demerara, on 12 August 1867. [St Andrews g/s]

COUPAR, JOHN, born 1848, from 2 Green Lawn, Rock Ferry, died in Monte Video on 1 May 1876. [S#10,261]

COUTTS, DAVID, born in Leven, Fife, during 1826, died in Calle Moreno 1232, Buenos Ayres, on 14 December 1878. [FH]

COUTTS, DAVID, dock manager at Callao, Peru, cnf Edinburgh 1896. [NAS.SC70.1.347/424]

COWAN, JANET, born 1806, died in Buenos Ayres in 1871. [SRP#365]

COWAN, THOMAS GRAHAM, in Demerara, cnf 1873 Edinburgh. [NAS.SC70.1.164/652]

COWAN, ..., son of T. Graham Cowan, was born in Georgetown, Demerara, on 9 December 1859. [CM#21619]

COWAN, MARGARET CECILIA JANE, daughter of Thomas Graham Cowan in Plantation Johanne Cecilia, Arabian Coast, Demerara, died at Rose Cottage, Braddan, Isle of Man, on 6 November 1876. [S#10,399]

CRAIG, AGNES JANE, daughter of Robert Robertson Craig, a skipper from Dundee, and his wife Agnes Robertson who were married in Dundee on 21 October 1853, was born on 21 May 1868 on the Southern Ocean in Callao Bay. [NRH/MRB]

CRAIG, JAMES, born in 1822, from Buckhaven, Fife, died in Guardia, Buenos Ayres, on 23 August 1888. [FFP]

CRAIG, MARGARET, eldest daughter of John H. Craig of Hudsco, married Henry L. Clayton, commander of the PSN Company's steamship Callao in Valparaiso on 20 January 1875. [EC#28226]

CRAIG, ROBERT, an engineer from Leven, Fife, father of daughters born in Tigre, Buenos Ayres, on 25 September 1871 and on 7 September 1873. [FH]

CRAIGEN, JAMES, born in Banffshire during 1832, died at Plantation Cornelia Ida, Demerara, on 20 December 1877. [AJ:29.1.1878]

CRAIGIE, JOHN, a sugar planter in Santiago, Argentina, cnf
Edinburgh 1892. [NAS.SC70.1.314/496]

CRAN, ANDREW, born in 1839, from Aberdeen, an overseer, died
at Rose Hall, Berbice, on 21 September 1865.
[AJ:25.10.1865]

CRAWFORD, CHARLES, born 1806, second son of Charles
Crawford in Portsoy, Banffshire, surgeon at the Military
Hospital, Proto Medico of the province of Chiriquanas, died in
Santa Cruz, Bolivia, during 1831. [AJ#4574]

CRAWFORD, FREDERICK AUGUSTUS BUCHAN, born in 1822,
son of John Crawford of Auchinames, died in Palmiras, Brazil,
on 9 November 1875. [EC#28455]

CRAWFORD, JAMES, in Demerara, 10 June 1859.
[NAS.RS.Edinburgh.74/5]

CRAWFORD, Mrs JOHANNA FREDERICA, in Havanna, Cuba, cnf
Edinburgh 1894. [NAS.SC70.1.330/391]

CRAWFORD, PETER, of Peter Crawford and Company, youngest
son of Charles Crawford in Portsoy, Banffshire, died in Tacna,
Upper Peru, on 1 June 1834. [AJ#4527]

CRAWFORD, ..., daughter of Joseph Tucker Crawford, HM
Consul in Tampico, born there on 19 March 1831. [PA#98]

CRAWFORD, ..., son of William Johnson Crawford, was born in
Monte Video on 28 March 1871. [S#8676]

CRAWFORD, ..., son of Johnson Crawford, was born in Monte
Video on 30 October 1874. [AO]

CRICHTON, DAVID, son of David Crichton a merchant in Dalkeith,
died in Demerara on 25 October 1802. [EA#4074.03]

CROMBIE, FRANCIS, from Edinburgh, died in Demerara on 24
April 1807. [SM#69.638]

CROSS, ALEXANDER, in Valparaiso, cnf 1878 Edinburgh.
[NAS.SC70.1.187/517]

CROSS, WALTER, son of Robert Cross an engineer in Glasgow,
settled as a merchant in Vera Cruz by 1836.
[NAS.SH.20.5.1836]

CROSSLEY, WILLIAM B., born 1845, a sugar planter, died on
Plantation Canefield, Berbice, in 1883. [S#12,622]

CROSSLEY, ..., son of William B. Crossley, was born at Plantation Camfield, Cauge Creek, Berbice, on 18 January 1880.[S#11,412]

CROSSLEY, ..., son of W. R.Crossley, was born at Plantation Canefield, Canje Creek, Berbice, British Guiana, on 29 January 1881. [S#11,735]

CRUICKSHANK, ALEXANDER, eldest son of Dr Cruickshank in Haughs of Corsie, died in Nickerie, Surinam, on 13 September 1820. [SM#86.383][S.4.195][AJ#4769]

CRUICKSHANK, ALEXANDER, of Strathcathro, died in Georgetown, Demerara, on 22 April 1846. [NAS.CC8.8.inv.1846]

CRUICKSHANK, DAVID CARRUTHERS, a druggist in Demerara, died 8 October 1855. Cnf 1856 Edinburgh [NAS.SC70.1.93/143]

CRUICKSHANK, JOHN, born 1863, educated at Glasgow University, MA 1885, minister of St James, British Guiana, 1896-1905, drowned 15 December 1905. [F.7.676]

CRUICKSHANK, ROBERT, third son of James S. Cruickshank, Logie Newton, Rothienorman, Aberdeenshire, died in New Amsterdam, Berbice, on 20 April 1900. [AJ:12.5.1900]

CRUICKSHANK, ..., daughter of William Cruickshank, was born at the Gasworks, Lima, Peru, 1 April 1870. [S#8360]

CULBARD, BERNARD, born 1856, died at San Pedro, Buenos Ayres, on 3 January 1885. [S#12976]

CUMING, ALEXANDER G., MD, born 1817, son of John Cuming a banker in Forres, Morayshire, died in Rio de Janeiro on 19 March 1845.[AJ#5135]

CUMMING, COLIN, from South America, married Janet Ness Henderson, in Kirkcaldy on 13 March 1883. [S#12,376]

CUMMING, JOHN, born 1806, died in Buenos Ayres in 1871. [SRP#365]

CUMING, LACHLAN, in Demerara, 24 January 1799. [NAS.RS.Elgin#494]; in Demerara, 1810. [GA.T-ARD#13/1]

CUMING, THOMAS, in Demerara, married Isabella, daughter of Colonel Fraser of Culladrum, there on 6 September 1798, [EA#3622.175]; in Demerara, husband of Isabella, daughter of Colonel James Fraser of Belladrum, 1798, [NAS.RD5.31.279];

in Demerara, 3 June 1799. [NAS.RS.Elgin & Forres, #508]; in Elgin late in Demerara, 1799, [NAS.GD23.6.364]; in Kelly, Demerara, 1800, [NAS.RD3.287.129/RD3.288.1]; release 1 April 1813 Moray, [NAS.CC16.9.10, 526]; in Elgin, late in Demerara, cnf 19 May 1813. [NAS.CC16.5.2.26][NAS.GD23.10.689]

CUMMING, THOMAS, in Demerara, graduated MD at Edinburgh University in 1824. [EUL]

CUMMING, THOMAS, in Demerara, 1858. [NAS.RS.Elgin#176]

CUMMING, THOMAS, born in 1873, son of Robert Cumming, 8 Ferryhill Place, Aberdeen, died in Para, Brazil, 4 June 1900. [AJ:2.7.1900]

CUNNINGHAM, CHARLOTTE, only daughter of Lieutenant Colonel Cunningham, HM Consul, married J. B. Boothby a merchant, in Bahia, Brazil, on 1 August 1816. [DPCA#743]

CUNNINGHAM, ROBERT, born 1808, son of Andrew Cunningham [1756-1819] and Jane McCraith [1783-1814], died in Talcahuano, Chile, 6 August 1877. [Barr g/s, Ayrshire]

CURCHEY, WILLIAM, born 1819, from Greenock, died in Valparaiso on 22 October 1853. [Greenock g/s, Renfrewshire]

CUTHBERT, ..., son of Thomas Cuthbert an engineer, was born in Coquimbo, Chile, on 23 November 1878. [S#11,074]

CUTHBERT,......, daughter of J. M. Cuthbert, was born and died on 27 August 1881 in Belize, British Honduras. [S#11,921]

CUTHBERT, ..., son of J. M. Cuthbert, was born in Belize on 30 November 1882. [S#12,308]

CUTHBERT,......, daughter of J. M. Cuthbert, was born in Belize on 23 March 1885. [S#13029]

CUTHBERTSON, GEORGE DOUGLAS, born 1851, a medical student from Inveresk, Musselburgh, youngest son of James Cuthbertson in Calcutta, died on Estancia de los Menrios, Pysander, Uruguay, on 24 January 1871. [S#8636]

CUTHBERTSON, MARGARET, wife of James Mackintosh a merchant in Buenos Ayres, died there on 29 January 1874. [S#9553]

CUTHILL, JOHN, an engineer, son of William Cuthill a merchant in Denny, Stirlingshire, died in Valparaiso on 20 February 1874. [EC#27938]

DALGETY, JAMES BOATH, born 20 September 1841 in Shandford Fearn, son of John Dalgety a farmer and his wife Margaret Sturrock, educated at Aberdeen University, minister of St Andrews, British Guiana, 1865-1869, of All Saints, Berbice, 1869-1876, died in Scotland 11 May 1908. [F.3.170]

DALGLEISH, Rev. JOHN, New Amsterdam, Berbice, married Catherine Fleming, eldest daughter of Rev. William Fleming in West Calder, Midlothian, in Georgetown, Demerara, on 24 November 1869. [S#7934]

DALGLEISH, Reverend JOHN, born 1812, died in New Amsterdam, Berbice, on 29 January 1884. [S#12,677]

DALGLEISH, THOMAS, son of Reverend John Dalgleish, married Alice Elizabeth Henderson, daughter of Reverend Thomas Henderson, in New Amsterdam, Berbice, on 6 March 1873. [S#9262]

DALZELL, COUTTS TROTTER, third son of Alexander Dalzell, died in Demerara on 31 January 1818. [BM#3.246]

DALZELL, HARRIET MARY, married Robert John Craig Christie, in Valparaiso on 14 May 1881. [S#11,849]

DAVIDSON, AGNES, daughter of John Davidson, Mains of Cairnbrogie, Tarves, married James B. Aiken of Callao, in Lima, on 2 September 1867. [AJ#6249]

DAVIDSON, ANDREW, born 1861, second son of James Davidson, Maryhill Street, Kirkcaldy, an engineer, died in Pisaqua, South America, on 4 August 1883. [FFP]

DAVIDSON, GEOFFREY WENTWORTH, in Argentina, cnf 1878 Edinburgh. [NAS.SC70.1.186/985]

DAVIDSON, JAMES, medical superintendent of the Patara Silver-Lead Mining Company, seventh son of Captain Hugh Davidson, Annan, Dumfries-shire, died at Pampa del Mirador, Chimlote, Peru, on 30 October 1883. [S#12,616]

DAVIDSON, JOHN, born 1869, son of William Davidson a farmer in Pittenkerrie, died in British Guina on 10 October 1893. [Banchory Ternan g/s][AJ:4.11.1893]

DAVIDSON, WILLIAM and JANE, transported from Surinam to Jamaica aboard the America in June 1675. [SPAWI.1675/285]

DAVIE, GEORGE, a timber merchant in Surinam, cnf 1875 Edinburgh. [NAS.SC70.1.174/1011]

DAVISON, ..., son of Henry Katz Davison, was born in New Amsterdam, British Guina, on 4 June 1872. [S#9007]

DAWSON, JOHN, a merchant from Aberdeen, died in Demerara on 17 February 1857. [AJ:17.6.1857]

DAWSON, THOMAS, married Margaret E. Young, daughter of James Cumming Young, a solicitor in Falmouth, in Rio de Janeiro on 13 April 1867. [S#7439]

DE MUNNICK, WILLIAM, late of Glasgow, died in Georgetown, Demerara, on 22 February 1839. [SG#8/761]

DENHOLM, THOMAS PATERSON, in Concordia Entre Rios, Argentina, cnf Edinburgh 1897. [NAS.SC70.1.359/317]

DENHOLM, WALTER, a sheep farmer, married Margaret, fourth daughter of Alexander Smith in Dunbar, East Lothian, on Estancia San Juan Paysandu, Monte Video, 5 October 1868. [S#7910]

DENHOLM, ..., daughter of Alexander Denholm, was born at Estancia San Juan, Paysandu, Monte Video, in 1867. [S#7559]

DENHOLM, ..., son of Alexander Denholm, was born on Estancia San Juan Paysandu, Monte Video, on 12 August 1868. [S#7860]

DENHOLM, ..., son of Walter Denholm, was born on Estancia San Juan Paysandu, Oriental, in 1870. [S#8498]

DENNISTON, JOHN ARCHIBALD, from Lima, Peru, eldest son of Archibald Denniston, WS in Greenock, married Rosetta Moyna, eldest daughter of James Moyna, of County Monaghan, Ireland, in Valparaiso, Chile, on 25 June 1873. [EC#27727][S#9379]

DENNISTON, ..., son of John A. Denniston, was born in Lima, Peru, 17 April 1874. [S#9599]

DE QUINCY, FRANCIS JOHN , MD, son of Thomas de Quincy, died in Brazil on 12 April 1861. [S#1870]

DEWAR, ANNIE, daughter of James Dewar, MD, in Kirkcaldy, Fife, and wife of William Duncan a surgeon, died in Essequibo, British Guiana, on 25 August 1882. [S#12,221]

DEWAR, NEIL WILLIAM, born 1860, of the firm of Dewar Brothers of Trinidad, died in Caracas, Venezuela, on 18 March 1883. [S#12,403]

DEWAR, ..., son of George Dewar a plantation manager, was born at Plantation Adelphi, Berbice, on 11 May 1868. [S#7763]

DIACK, ALEXANDER, born 1800, emigrated from Cromarty on the Planet of London, Captain William Barclay, on 1 October 1825, landed at La Guayra on 2 December 1825, superintendent of the colony at Topo. [PRO.FO.18/47; FO.199/3/32]

DICK, DAVID, second son of Alexander Dick an accountant in Edinburgh, died in Alvarada, Mexico, during November 1825. [EA#6493.111]

DICK, Reverend JAMES, born 1861, youngest son of James Dick in Rankeillor, Fife, a missionary, died in Ceara, Brazil, on 21 April 1892. [PJ]

DICK, JOHN, born 1854, only son of Robert Dick in Prinlaws, Leslie, Fife, died in San Paulo, Brazil, on 14 November 1886. [PJ]

DICKSON, GEORGE TAIT, B.M., in British Guiana, cnf 1882 Edinburgh. [NAS.SC70.1.217/407]

DICKSON, JOHN, son of Gilbert Dickson in Glasgow, died in Demerara on 6 December 1808. [SM#71.238]

DINGWALL, DONALD, 47, late in Demerara, died 6 January 1817(?). [Dingwall g/s]

DODD, ROBERT YOUNG, in Puerto Rico, cnf 1869 Edinburgh. [NAS.SC70.1.143/44]

DODD, THOMAS ANDERSON, an engineer in Pouce, Puerto Rico, cnf Edinburgh 1897. [NAS.SC70.1.364/299]

DODD, WILLIAM ANDERSON, in Puerto Rico, cnf 1869 Edinburgh. [NAS.SC70.1.143/40]

DODDS, CATHERINE, born 1839, from Berwickshire, died in Buenos Ayres in 1871. [SRP#365]

DONALD, JAMES, born 1822, son of David Donald and Elizabeth Whitehead, died at Patook off the Musquito Coast 27 August 1852. [Kinnoull g/s, Perthshire]

DONALDSON, JOHN PATON, born in 1872, eldest son of Alexander Donaldson a skipper in Aberdeen, died in Campinas, Brazil, on 1 March 1892. [AJ:29.3.1892]

DOUGLAS, A. F., born 1854, died in Buenos Ayres in 1871. [SRP#365]

DOUGLAS, ADAM, youngest son of Adam T. Douglas from Moneylaws, died in Buenos Ayres on 13 April 1871. [S#8677]

DOUGLAS, AGNES CASE, daughter of Colin Douglas in Demerara, married John Torbet, a surgeon in Paisley, in Limehouse, London, on 21 July 1828. [S#893.490]

DOUGLAS, ANDREW, a merchant in Surinam, inventory 21 January 1706 New York. [NY Wills, liber 3-4, fo.453-455]

DOUGLAS, COLIN, died in Demerara on 27 February 1827. [EA#6615.255]

DOUGLAS, HUGH, merchant in Demerara, co-owner of the Nancy of Glasgow, 1799. [NAS.CE60.11.6/80]

DOUGLAS, JAMES, second son of James Douglas accountant of the Commercial Bank in Edinburgh, died in Paramaribo, Surinam, 7 November 1874. [S#9785]

DOUGLAS, ROBERT, born in Aberdeen around 1745, settled in the West Indies and on the Mosquito Shore for 50 years, former Treasurer of the English settlement on the Bay of Honduras, died in Hutchesontown, Glasgow, during 1827. [SM#22.768]

DOUGLAS, ROBERT, in Honduras, married Margaret, daughter of William Watson in Abbotsinch, in Hutchesontown on 4 October 1813. [SM#75.878]

DOUGLAS, ROBERT, a sugar planter on Better Hope Estate, Demerara, died at 25 India Street, Edinburgh, on 26 April 1826, cnf 1864 Edinburgh. [BM#19.766]

DOUGLAS, ROBERT, a sugar planter in Demerara, cnf 1868 Edinburgh. [NAS.SC70.1.141/301]

DOW, ROBERT RAMSAY, captain of the brig James of London, son of J.B.Dow in Leith, died in Honduras during 1853. [EEC#22500]

DOW, Mrs, emigrated from Cromarty on the Planet of London, Captain William Barclay, on 1 October 1825, landed at La Guayra on 2 December 1825, settled at Topo, Columbia, by 1827. [PRO.FO.18/47; FO.199/3/32]

DOWNIE, DAVID, son of William Downie a gilder in St Andrews, Fife, died in Guadaloupe Hospital, Callao, on 11 May 1869. [FA]

DOWNIE, ELIZABETH, youngest daughter of James Downie from Leith, died in Valparaiso, Chile, on 12 March 1869. [S#8059]

DOWNIE, JAMES, an engineer, married Jane Sinclair, eldest daughter of John Sinclair in North Leith, in Valparaiso on 6 August 1862. [S#2276]

DOWNIE, JAMES, only son of James Downie from Leith, died in Valparaiso, Chile, on 12 March 1869. [S#8059]

DOWNIE, ..., daughter of James Downie, was born in Valparaiso, Chile, on 2 June 1863. [S#2534]

DOWNIE, ..., son of James Downie, was born at Pasaje de Quillota, Valparaiso, on 21 February 1873. [S#9274]

DOWNIE, ..., son of James Downie, was born at El Pasaje de Quillota, Valparaiso, Chile, on 12 November 1876. [S#10,440]

DRON, JOHN, shipmaster in Valparaiso, cnf 1882. [NAS.SC70.1.218/166]

DRUMMOND, THOMAS, in South America, 1848. [NAS.RD5.804.175]

DRUMMOND, WILLIAM WALKER, a mine manager in Mirador, Peru, cnf 1884 Edinburgh. [NAS.SC70.1.237/127]

DRYBURGH, ALEXANDER, a carpenter and mariner, died in Demerara on 26 July 1852, cnf 1853 Edinburgh [NAS.CC8.8.inv.1853]

DRYSDALE, ALFRED T., from Glasgow, married Maude Morton from North Kensington, in St Andrew's Scots Church, Buenos Ayres, on 11 January 1899. [S#17334]

DRYSDALE, JOHN, born 2 July 1833, died in Buenos Ayres on 22 March 1893. [Prestonkirk g/s]

DRYSDALE,...., son of Juan Drysdale, was born in Buenos Ayres on 27 June 1884. [S#12,785]

DUDGEON, JOHN, a shipmaster at the Bay of Honduras in 1792. [NAS.RS.Glasgow#1688]

DUFF, ALEXANDER, son of Reverend David Duff in Kenmore, Perthshire, died in Georgetown, Demerara, on 16 August 1877.[EC#28980][S#10,648]

DUFF, ROBERT, born 1810, son of Robert Duff, farmer in Milton of Buchromb, and Elizabeth Gordon, educated at King's College, Aberdeen, in 1828, a minister in Berbice, died in New Amsterdam in 1878. [KCA#284][F.7.673/678]

DUGUID, GEORGE, born during 1783, died on Orangestein Estate, Essequibo, on 7 January 1807. [SM#69.798][DPCA#269]

DUGUID, JOHN, son of Thomas Duguid a merchant in Buenos Ayres, educated at Marischal College, Aberdeen, in 1841. [MCA#2.514]

DUGUID, Mrs THOMAS, died in Buenos Ayres on 17 May 1837. [AJ#4677]

DUGUID, THOMAS, born in 1798, late of Buenos Ayres, died in Liverpool, England, on 24 January 1875. [EC#28181]

DUGUID, WILLIAM FRANCIS, in Buenos Ayres, married Jessie Bothwell Fraser, youngest daughter of John Fraser in Liverpool, in Buenos Ayres on 11 November 1874. [S#9797]

DUN, JAMES, born in Montrose, Angus, during 1805, died in Buenos Ayres on 23 March 1848. [AJ#5243]

DUNCAN, JOHN, born in 1821, son of John Fraser in Cullen, died in Georgetown, Demerara, on 31 May 1837. [AJ:16.8.1837]

DUNCAN, JOHN, third son of John Duncan in Cullen, died in Georgetown, Demerara, on 31 May 1837. [AJ#4675]

DUNCAN, ROBERT, from Greenock, died on Plantation Tuscheu de Vrieden, Demerara, on 10 November 1838. [SG#8/740]

DUNCAN, ROBERT, born 1831, late of Fales and Duncan, merchants in Rio de Janeiro, eldest son of Thomas Duncan a brush manufacturer in Edinburgh, died in Rio de Janeiro on 16 June 1876. [S#10,287]

DUNCAN, THOMAS, from Coxton, died in Demerara on 6 May 1821. [S#240.272]

DUNCAN, WILLIAM, a merchant in Berbice, died on 21 April 1814. [EC#621]

DUNCAN, WILLIAM, born 1831, younger son of Peter Duncan, Westfield, Linlithgow, West Lothian, died in La Noria, Iquique, Peru, on 27 January 1879. [S#11,129]

DUNCAN,......, manager for J. Honeyman and Company in Pathhead, Fife, emigrated to Buenos Ayres in March 1897. [FFP, 27.3.1897]

DUNDAS, ..., son of Charles S. Dundas, HM Consul in Santos, Brazil, was born in Rio de Janeiro on 25 June 1873. [EC#27718]

DUNDAS, ..., daughter of C. S. Dundas, was born in Santos, Brazil, in 1876. [EC#28541]

DUNLOP, COLIN, a merchant in Demerara, 1821, brother of William Dunlop a mariner in Port Glasgow, eldest son of William Dunlop a shipmaster in Port Glasgow. [NAS.CS17.1.40/183]

DUNN, JANET, in Pernambuco, died in September 1844, cnf Edinburgh 1846. [NAS.CC8.8.inv.1846]

DUNLOP,....., son of George Dunlop, master of the <u>Zeeburg</u>, and his wife Christian Hope Lyle, was born in Valparaiso on 13 November 1879. [S#11,379]

DUNN, JOHN, born 1855, son of Alexander C. Dunn engineer in Holytown, died in Brazil on 3 May 1871. [S#8682]

DUNN, WILLIAM R., born in Huntly, Aberdeenshire, during 1857, died in Georgetown, Demerara, on 2 July 1884. [AJ:29.7.1884]

DUNSMURE, JAMES HENDERSON, a farmer at Sandy Point, South America, cnf 1882 Edinburgh. [NAS.SC70.1.218/306]

DUTHIE, JOHN, born 1840, from Aberdeen, a carpenter on the City of Glasgow, died in Demerara on 24 November 1866. [AJ:16.1.1867]

DYKES, JAMES, manager of James Lade and Company, died in New Amsterdam, Berbice, on 30 July 1873. [EC#27737]

EASTON, Reverend ANDREW ALEXANDER, minister of St Mary's, Demerara, third son of Reverend Dr Easton of Kirriemuir, Angus, died at St Mary's on 28 December 1859, cnf 1860 Edinburgh. [AJ#5853][NAS.SC70.1.104/1015][S#1474][F.7.678]

EASTON, JAMES GARDINER, born 1820, son of John Easton and Martha Gardiner, died in Valparaiso on 19 August 1847. [Luncarty g/s, Perthshire]

EASTON, ROBERT, from Demerara, graduated at Leyden University 26 March 1830. [LUL]

EASTON, WILLIAM, a merchant, youngest son of Thomas Easton a painter in Dunbar, East Lothian, died in Monte Video on 12 August 1879. [S#11,296]

EDINGTON, THOMAS, a merchant in Valparaiso, cnf 1871 Edinburgh. [NAS.SC70.1.155/21]

EDMONSTONE, CHARLES, in Demerara, later in Broadfield, 1822. [NAS.CS17.1.41/277]

ELDER, HENRY, an engineer from Edinburgh, died in Lima, Peru, on 1 August 1879. [S#11,283]

ELLIOT, ROBERT, in Demerara, 1779. [NAS.RD4.235.748]

ELMSLIE, ELIZABETH MCCOMBIE, born in 1853, daughter of Peter Elmslie in Huntly, Aberdeenshire, and wife of Francis Leys, died in Buenos Ayres on 12 July 1878. [EC#29293]

ERSKINE, C. W. T., a writer from Glasgow, died in Belize on 24 December 1838. [SG#8/753]

EWART, JAMES THOMSON, born 1879, youngest son of Robert Ewart late of Blairshinnoch, Dumfries-shire, died at 383 Calle Bolivar, Buenos Ayres, on 11 March 1898. [AO: 22.4.1898]

EWING, JOHN, son of Duncan Ewing and Isabella Buchanan, died in Rio de Janeiro on 27 September 1826. [Greenock West g/s]

EWING, WILLIAM, a planter in Demerara, 1811. [NAS.SC58.59.2.62]; later in Greenock, cnf 16 July 1811 Glasgow. [NAS.CC9.7.77.361]

FAIR, MARY JANE, youngest daughter of Thomas Fair in Buenos Ayres, and widow of Lewis S.Thomas in Bombay, died 2 July 1884. [S#12803]

FAIR, THOMAS, a merchant, married Harriott Kendall, in Buenos Ayres on 29 March 1818. [BM#3.628]

FAIR, THOMAS, junior, born 1823, son of Thomas Fair in Hope Crescent, Edinburgh, late in Buenos Ayres, drowned on his father's estate of San Jorge, Rio Negro, Banda Oriental, on 7 November 1853. [EEC#22540]

FAIR, ..., son of James Fair, was born in Monte Video on 30 April 1861. [S#1867]

FAIR, ..., son of James Fair, was born in Buenos Ayres on 25 November 1866. [S#7308]

FAIR, ..., son of George Fair MD, was born in Buenos Ayres on 1 February 1874. [S#9579]

FAIRBAIRN, WILLIAM JOHN, MD, in Rio de Janeiro, cnf Edinburgh 1892. [NAS.SC70.1.311/235]

FAIRBAIRN, ..., son of William J. Fairbairn MD, was born in Rio de Janeiro on 31 March 1867. [S#7426]

FALCONER, JOHN, in Topo, Columbia, before 1825

FARQUHARSON, ANDREW, in Demerara, 1796. [NAS.RH1.2.852]

FERGUSON, ALEXANDER, minister of St Luke's, British Guiana, 1856-1868. [F.7.677]

FERGUSON, ELEANOR ISOBEL, eldest daughter of David Ferguson in Mexico, married William Neobold, in Mexico City on 24 August 1877. [EC#29028]

FERGUSON Mrs EMILY, wife of Colonel Ferguson, died in Mexico on 8 May 1875. [EC#28304]

FERGUSON, JOHN, late in Essequibo now in Stranraer, 1821. [NAS.CS17.1.40/393]; cnf 29 October 1821 Wigtown

FERGUSON, JOHN, from Edinburgh, late apprentice to Muir Wood and Company, musical instrument makers and music sellers in Edinburgh, now in Rio de Janeiro, 1822. [NAS.CS17.1.41/319]

FERGUSON, MARGARET JANE, wife of David Dick MacFarlane, died in Valparaiso on 16 October 1868. [S#7920]

FERGUSON, MARTIN PATERSON, born on 16 June 1826, son of John Ferguson a merchant in Kilmarnock, Ayrshire, and Elizabeth Muir, a minister in Argentina from 1862, died 2 September 1906. [F.7.681]

FERGUSON, WILLIAM, born 1854, fifth son of William Ferguson of Charlotte Street, Leith, was drowned near Vera Cruz on 6 February 1872. [S#9002]

FERGUSON, ..., son of William Ferguson a merchant from Lanark, died in Valparaiso on 11 April 1869. [S#8070]

FERGUSON, ... daughter of William Ferguson from Lanark, was born in Valparaiso on 5 May 1871. [S#8686]

FERNIE, ANDREW, eldest son of James Blyth Fernie of Kilmux, died in Valparaiso on 27 November 1874. [EC#28171]; cnf 1875 Edinburgh. [NAS.SC70.1.173/861]

FERRIER, ALEXANDER, Bloomhill, Dunbartonshire, late in Surinam, died 20 April 1848, cnf 1849 Edinburgh

FERRIER, HUGH, settled in Aquadilla, Porto Rico, by 1836. [NAS.SH.21.6.1836]

FINLAY, JOHN J., born 1851, died in Mexico City on 17 February 1887. [People's Journal]

FINLAYSON, JOHN ADAM, born in Dingwall 1833, grandson of Roderick Finlayson (1812-1889) and Catherine McKenzie (1812-1902), died in Buenos Ayres 1907. [Dingwall g/s]

FINLAYSON, MARY ALLEN, daughter of William Allen in Mile-end, Aberdeen, died in Fredericksburg, Demerara, on 22 January 1866. [AJ:14.3.1866]

FINNIE, ARCHIBALD, late of Rio de Janeiro, died in London on 3 May 1885. [S#13047]

FINNIE, JOHN, son of Archibald Finnie [1746-1826] and Janet Muir [1749-1822], settled in Rio de Janeiro, later in Kilmarnock, 1838. [Kilmarnock g/s, Ayrshire] [NAS.RS.Glasgow#5833]

FINNIE, ROBERT, born in 1783, son of Archibald Finnie [1746-1826] and Janet Muir [1749-1822], settled in Rio de Janeiro, died during1831 in London. [Kilmarnock g/s, Ayrshire]

FINNIE, WILLIAM, of Finnie Brothers merchants in Rio de Janeiro, eldest son of William Finnie in Kilmarnock, Ayrshire, died in Rio de Janeiro on 20 April 1849. [SG#18/1833]

FITZGERALD, THOMAS, in Para, Brazil, cnf Edinburgh 1898. [NAS.SC70.1.369/747]

FLEMING, CATHERINE, eldest daughter of Rev. William Fleming in West Calder, Midlothian, married Rev. John Dalgleish, New Amsterdam, Berbice, in Georgetown, Demerara, on 24 November 1869. [S#7934]

FLEMING JAMES WILLIAM, born in Ballindalloch, Inveraven, on 28 August 1855, son of John Fleming and Ann Gardner, educated at Aberdeen University and at Edinburgh University, a minister in Buenos Ayres, Argentina, from 1879, died 14 June 1925. [F.7.681]

FLEMING, THOMAS, an engineer, son of George Fleming, Edenbank, St Andrews, Fife, died in Georgetown, Demerara, on 4 December 1853. [FH]

FLETCHER, ..., born in Berbice on 14 December 1805. [SM#68.155]

FORBES, ALEXANDER, merchant and author in Tepic, Mexico, around 1839. [NLS]

FORBES, ALEXANDER, born in 1830, son of John Forbes and Jean Dick, died in Berbice, British Guina, on 23 October 1876. [Anstruther Easter g/s]

FORBES, Reverend FRANCIS, born in Old Machar, Aberdeen, 27 September 1804, son of Dr Patrick Forbes of King's College, Aberdeen, educated at King's College, Aberdeen, MA 1821, minister of St Luke's, Demerara, British Guiana, died 8 December 1855. [KCA#278][AJ#5636][F.7.677]

FORBES, JAMES, born in 1799, son of John Forbes a merchant in Inverness, resident in Demerara for 16 years, died there on 29 December 1830. [AJ#4338]

FORBES, JOHN, of Skellatur, born 1732, Governor of Rio de Janeiro, died there on 8 April 1808. [AJ.Obits.]

FORBES, WILLIAM, in Kingston, Jamaica, 1733. [NAS,GD23.6.105]

FORD, ..., daughter of Frederick Ford, was born in Lima, Peru, on 25 September 1875. [EC#28419]

FORBES, ... daughter of Edmond B. Forbes, M. Inst. C.E., was born in Taital, Chile, on 21 March 1899. [S#17,395]

FORREST, JAMES, from Bowhousebog, Shotts, Lanarkshire, died in Monte Video 24 July 1870. [S#8450]

FORRESTER, JOHN, in Corosal, Honduras, cnf 1872 Edinburgh. [NAS.SC70.1.157/159]

FORSYTH, ROBERT, born in 1788, a merchant who died in Rio de Janeiro on 31 July 1811. [DPCA#483]

FOULIS, ROBERT, second son of Sir William Liston Foulis, died in the English Hospital, Buenos Ayres, in February 1874. [EC#27930]

FOWLER, ALPIN GRANT, eldest son of Reverend James Fowler in Urquhart, Inverness-shire, married Ann Margaret Thomson, only daughter of Dr Robert Thomson in Demerara, at Georgetown, Demerara, on 13 June 1838. [AJ#4727]

FRANKLAND, THOMAS, in Demerara 1810. [NAS.RD2.310.691]

FRASER, ALEXANDER or ANGUS, brother of William Fraser of Balnain, in Mexico during 1760s. [NAS.NRAS.0002]

FRASER, ANGUS, born in 1782, a merchant in Demerara, died between Berbice and Demerara on 20 April 1814. [EC#620]

FRASER, ANGUS, in Demerara, son of Alexander Fraser of Ballindern, Inverness-shire, an inventory 1839. [NAS.GD23.10.732]

FRASER, DANIEL, a commission agent and merchant in NY, second son of Robert Fraser of Kilcoy in Berbice, formerly a merchant in Inverness, died in Thompsonville, Connecticut, 22 August 1869. [S#8150]

FRASER, HARRY, in Tacopilla, Chile, son of Reverend Henry Erskine Fraser in Edinburgh who died 15 May 1890. [NAS.SH.17.7.1896]

FRASER, HUGH FORSYTH, second son of J. Fraser a schoolmaster in Carluke, Lanarkshire, died in Tijuca, Rio de Janeiro, 16 February 1869. [S#8005]

FRASER, JAMES, in Berbice, 1801, probate PCC 15 August 1801

FRASER, JAMES, son of James Fraser of Belladrum, Inverness-shire, a planter in Demerara, 1795. [NAS.GD23.5.352]

FRASER, JAMES, of Belladrum, in Berbice 1808. [NAS.GD23.10.663]

FRASER, JAMES, in Demerara, 1829. [NAS.SH.9.10.1829]

FRASER, JAMES, MD, late of Demerara, died in Innerleithen, Peebles-shire, on 27 November 1868. [S#7904]

FRASER, JAMES, a draper, born 1855, second son of William Fraser, a butler in Pitmilly, Fife, died in Georgetown, Demerara, on 9 May 1881. [PJ]

FRASER, JAMES HENRY MANSEL, born in 1847, son of Major J. Fraser of the 60th Rifles, died in Rossario, Argentina, on 6 May 1878. [EC#29249]

FRASER, JOHN DENHOLM, a Stipendiary Magistrate in Demerara, youngest son of William Fraser in Melrose, married Johanna Bishop, daughter of Edward Bishop of Plantation Zorg, in Essequibo 22 May 1849. [EEC#21832]

FRASER JOHN DUNCAN, born 1820, third son of John Fraser in Cullen, Banffshire, died in Georgetown, Demerara, 31 May 1837. [AJ#4675]

FRASER, JOHN G., in Demerara 1807. [NAS.GD23.6.427]

FRASER, JOHN, born 1836, son of Thomas Fraser in Clachnaharry and his wife Ann Wishart, died in Georgetown, Demerara, on 29 December 1866. [Old High Church g/s, Inverness]

FRASER, JOHN, in Glasgow, late in Callao, cnf Edinburgh 1898. [NAS.SC70.1.375/156]

FRASER, JOHANNA, wife of James D. Fraser a stipendiary magistrate, died in Georgetown, Demerara, 27 March 1861. [S#1828]

FRASER, JOHN, late in Demerara, cnf 1821 Edinburgh. [NAS.SC70.1.25/62]

FRASER, MALCOLM, born in 1839, youngest son of Alexander Fraser, Albany Street Lane, Edinburgh, died in Buenos Ayres on 6 September 1878. [EC#29338][S#10,990]

FRASER, SIMON, eldest son of Donald Fraser of Balloan, settled on the Golden Fleece Plantation in Berbice, died in Berbice on 15 September 1803. [DPCA#72]

FRASER, SUSAN, eldest daughter of Simon Fraser of Kilmorack, married W. Katz, in Berbice on 9 January 1826. [EA]

FRASER, WILLIAM, a planter in Berbice, 1818. [NAS.CS96/2130/1]

FRASER, WILLIAM, youngest son of Reverend Thomas Fraser in Inverness, died in Henrietta, Demerara, on 2 November 1881. [Dingwall, St Clement, g/s]

FRASER, WILLIAM, second son of Donald Fraser in Strathpeffer, died in Demerara on 1 November 1881. [S#11,977]

FREEMAN,THOMAS GODFREY, eldest son of Thomas J. Freeman of H.M. Customs in Leith, died at Fray Bentos, on the River Plate, on 23 June 1872. [S#9067]

FRISLIN, MARY CATHERINE, born 1797, died in Demerara on 15 January 1815. [Edinburgh, Greyfriars g/s]

FULLARTON, ALEXANDER, a merchant in Demerara, co-owner of the Maria of Greenock, 1801, [NAS.CE60.11.7/76]; died in Demerara on 1 October 1818. [S#98.18]

FULLARTON, JOHN, in Glasgow, partner in Fullarton and forster merchants in Demerara, 1804. [NAS.AC7/77]; a merchant in Demerara, 1817. [NAS.RS54.GR205/127]

FYFE, JAMES, youngest son of Captain Fyfe of the Royal Navy in Portsoy, Banffshire, died on Plantation Prospect, Berbice, on 17 September 1847. [AJ#5263]

GALBRAITH, Reverend PETER, born 1836, minister of St Catherine's, died in New Amsterdam, British Guiana, on 3 February 1884. [S#12,688]

GALBRAITH, THOMAS, born 1797, a farmer, with his wife Jane and a child, emigrated from Leith to Argentina on the Symmetry, master William Cochrane, on 22 May 1825. [SSP#18]

GALL, ROGER, merchant at the Bay of Honduras 1775. [NAS.RD4.228.1092]

GALLETLY, ALEXANDER JOHN, born 1851, eldest son of John Galletly, SSC, Edinburgh, died in Guaymas, Mexico, on 10 September 1878. [S#11,000]

GAUGAIN, JAMES THOMAS, born 1824, eldest son of John James Gaugain in Edinburgh, died in Mexico 1847. [SG#17/1700]

GEBBIE, ALBERT GEORGE VALLANCE, in Buenos Ayres, cnf Edinburgh 1896. [NAS.SC70.1.350/320]

GEBBIE, Reverend FRANCIS, born on 13 May 1831 in Maxwood, Galston, Ayrshire, fourth son of John Gebbie, a farmer, and Ellen Smith, educated at Glasgow University, minister of St John's, Quilmes, Buenos Ayres, from 1857 to 1883, died at 2 Murrayfield Avenue, Edinburgh, on 16 December 1918. [F#7.681] [Dean g/s, Edinburgh]

GEBBIE, WILLIAM SMITH, son of John Gebbie (1776-1862) and Helen Smith (1794-1838), died in Buenos Ayres in March 1873. [Galston g/s, Ayrshire]

GELLATLY, WILLIAM, born 1842, son of John Gellatly an engraver in Edinburgh, died in Santiago, Chile, on 13 May 1869. [S#8059]

GELLION, THOMAS, born in 1820, son of Thomas Gellion {1781-1840} and Helen McKinnon {1782-1829}, died in Berbice on 26 August 1837. [Chapel Yard g/s, Inverness]

GENTLE, ALEXANDER, third son of Alexander Gentle in Dunkeld, Perthshire, died in Demerara on 17 December 1818. [S#62.18]

GENTLE, JAMES, in Demerara 1814. [NAS.RD5.182.697]

GENTLE, WILLIAM, in Honduras, 1828. [NAS.RD5.392.594]

GENTLE, WILLIAM, in Belize, cnf 1875 Edinburgh. [NAS.SC70.1.173/1083]

GENTLE, WILLIAM, son of William Gentle, was born in Belize, Honduras, on 5 July 1867. [S#7490]; died there 15 May 1868. [S#7767]

GENTLE, ..., son of William Gentle, was born in Belize, Honduras, on 28 June 1868. [S#7799]; William, youngest son of William Gentle, died in Belize in June 1873. [S#9352]

GENTLE, ..., daughter of William Gentle, was born in Belize, Honduras, 7 November 1870. [S#8560]

GENTLE, ..., son of William Gentle, was born in Belize, Honduras, 13 April 1874. [S#9613]

GIBB, WILLIAM, born 1839, son of George Gibb [1809-1847] and Margaret McLean [1815-1879], died in Demerara on 27 Aug.1859. [Barr, Ayrshire, g/s]

GIBBON, ISABELLA, second daughter of James Gibbon in Aberdeen, married Alexander Morice a merchant, in Rio de Janeiro on 8 July 1809. [SM#72.798]

GIBBS, ARCHIBALD ROBERTSON, married Eliza Phillips in Belize on 23 May 1867. [S#7502]

GIBSON, GEORGE, from Glasgow, a cattle breeder in Sanborombon, Argentina, 1834-1838. [NLS.MS10326/110]

GIBSON, JAMES, eldest son of Major James Gibson of the Dunbarton Fencibles, and grandson of James Gibson a surgeon in Edinburgh, died in Berbice on 7 November 1807. [SM#70.398]

GIBSON, or MACKENZIE, JEMIMA MARGARET, daughter of Reverend Dr James Gibson, of Avoch, widow of D. W. Mackenzie, died in Fray Bentos, Uruguay, on 1 January 1883, cnf 1883 Edinburgh. [NAS.SC70.1.24/323][S#12,348]

GIBSON, JOHN, a merchant in Demerara, died 7 December 1857. Cnf 1858 Edinburgh

GIBSON, MARGARET DRYSDALE, born 8 May 1830, died in Buenos Ayres on 31 July 1896, buried in Chacanta, Buenos Ayres. [Prestonkirk g/s]

GIBSON, PATRICK, a merchant, married Jessie Baillie, eldest daughter of Thomas Bisset Baillie MD, in Arequibo, Peru, on 22 April 1849. [SG#18/1847]

GIBSON, ROBERT, from Glasgow, a rancher in Buenos Ayres, 1836-1842. [NLS.ms10326/158]

GIBSON, ROBERT FORREST, born 1859, second son of John Gibson a fishcurer in Fisherrow, Musselburgh, died in Rio de Janeiro on 20 March 1876. [S#10,229]

GIBSON, THOMAS, from Glasgow, a cattle and sheep breeder in Ajo, Argentina, around 1850. [NLS.ms10326/1]

GIBSON, ..., daughter of Ernest Gibson, was born at Los Ynglesias, Ajo, Buenos Ayres, on 14 February 1899. [S#17,363]

GILBERT, EBENEZER, in Demerara, cnf 1870 Edinburgh.
[NAS.SC70.1.148/749]
GILBERT, PATRICK in Georgetown, Demerara, cnf 1878
Edinburgh. [NAS.SC70.1.188/759]
GILLANDERS, THOMAS, born 1802, second son of George
Gillanders in Lewis, died in Buenos Ayres in December 1831.
[AJ#4411]
GILLIES, DONALD, with his wife, and children John born 1806,
Donald born 1809, Duncan born 1813, Margaret born 1818,
and Angus born 1820, emigrated from Cromarty on the Planet
of London, Captain William Barclay, on 1 October 1825,
landed at La Guayra on 2 December 1825, settled at Topo,
Columbia, by 1827. [PRO.FO.18/47; FO.199/3/32]
GILMOUR, ANN, only daughter of Thomas Gilmour in Buenos
Ayres, died in Markinch, Fife, on 15 January 1852. [FJ]
GILMORE, JOHN, an engineer from Burntisland, Fife, in Santiago,
Chile, 1891. [NAS.RS.Burntisland.13/264]
GILMORE, ROBERT, from Burntisland, Fife, an engineer in Callao,
Peru, 1898. [NAS.RS.Burntisland.16.45]
GILMORE, ROBERT, jr., from Burntisland, Fife, an engineer in
Callao, Peru, 1898. [NAS.RS.Burntisland.13.265]
GILZEAN, ALEXANDER RUSSELL, of Tuschen-de-Vrienden,
married Eliza W. Kelly, second daughter of Robert George
Kelly of Claughton, Birkenhead, and granddaughter of R. N.
Kelly, R.N., in British Guiana on 30 April 1878. [S#10,887]
GLADSTONE, ROBERT, an engineer in Rio de Janeiro, cnf 1871
Edinburgh. [NAS.SC70.1.151/454]
GLADSTONE, WILLIAM, minister in British Guina, died in
November 1836. [F.7.678]
GLASGOW, WILLIAM, born 1833, died in Campana, Buenos
Ayres, on 17 April 1879. [S#11,204]
GLEGG, JANE, only daughter of Robert Glegg of H.M.Exchequer in
Edinburgh, married David Stewart Ramsay Gordon, eldest
son of Samuel Gordon, Woodside, Brechin, Angus, in
Valparaiso, Chile, on 7 November 1877. [S#10,739]
GLENNIE, ..., daughter of Charles A. Glennie, was born in Santos,
Brazil, on 25 September 1850. [AJ#5387]

GOLDIE, THOMAS DICKSON, born in 1799 sixth son of James Goldie in Bonnyrig, Midlothian, died in Demerara on 1 December 1820. [BM#8.708]

GOODFELLOW, JOHN, born during 1800 son of Thomas Goodfellow and Catherine Farquharson, died in New Granada during 1860. [Ceres, Fife, g/s]

GOODFELLOW, ROBERT LEYDEN, in Buenos Ayres, cnf Edinburgh 1901. [NAS.SC70.1.405/61]

GOODFELLOW, WILLIAM, fourth son of Alexander Goodfellow of Headshaw, Ashkirk parish, Roxburghshire, married Maggie Harrow, youngest daughter of John Harrow from Paisley, in Buenos Ayres on 25 April 1873. [S#9326]

GORDON, CHARLES, MD, from Pernambuco, Brazil, married Bertha, youngest daughter of Michael F. Gordon of Abergeldie, Aberdeenshire, at Gittisham, Devon, on 4 October 1855. [EEC#322801]

GORDON, DAVID STEWART RAMSAY, eldest son of Samuel Gordon of Woodside, Brechin, Angus, married Jane Glegg, only daughter of Robert Glegg of H.M. Exchequer in Edinburgh, in Valparaiso, Chile, on 7 November 1877. [S#10,739]

GORDON, GEORGE, and his son George Gordon jr., transported from Surinam to Jamaica on <u>HMS Hercules</u> in June 1675. [SPAWI.1675/285]

GORDON, GEORGE, President of the Berbice Court of Justice, died in Berbice 15 November 1820. [GM.91.185]

GORDON, HUNTLY, third daughter of William Gordon in Aberdeen, married Peter Ross from Demerara, in London on 16 June 1820. [BM#7.462]

GORDON, JAMES, in Demerara, dead by 1807. [GA.T-ARD#13/1]

GORDON, JAMES MUTER ANDERSON, born in 1845, an engineer who died at St John d'el Rey Company Mines, Murra Vilho, Minas Geraes, Brazil, on 12 June 1875. [EC#28344]

GORDON, JOHN, Huntly Plantation, Demerara, and Litchfield Plantation, Berbice, 1811. [NAS.GD23.6.484]

GORDON, JOHN SUTHERLAND, born in 1821, a planter in Enmore, Demerara, married Mary Gowans, sixth daughter of

George Gowans in Cawdor, Nairnshire, in Demerara on 25 April 1863, died on 19 August 1880. [S#2482][Burntisland g/s]

GORDON, MADELINA, fourth daughter of William Gordon of Aberlour, married John Murray McGusty in Georgetown Demerara, on 20 June 1825. [S#587.543]

GORDON, PETER, at Plantation Borlum, Berbice, dead by 1809. [NAS.GD23.7.39]

GORDON, ROBERT, in Demerara, 1801. [NAS.RS38.GR635.56]

GORDON, ROBERT, of Hope Estate, Demerara, married Ann Parkinson on 3 June 1804. [SM#66.806]

GORDON, ROBERT, Huntley Estate, Demerara, before 1815. [NLS.Acc4644]

GORDON, Dr WILLIAM, second son of John Gordon of Carroll, died in Demerara on 7 January 1817. [S#7.17]

GORRIE, WILLIAM, born in 1842, son of David Gorrie and Barbara Bett, died in Rio de Janeiro on 26 September 1872. [Ferryport-on-Craig g/s, Fife]

GOULD, WILLIAM, from Glasgow, Lieutenant of the 5th West Indian Regiment, died in Berbice, Bay of Honduras, 11 May 1801. [GM.72.181]

GOW, GEORGE, an engineer from Aberdeenshire, died in Campinas, Sao Paulo, Brazil, on 4 March 1892. [AJ:2.4.1897]

GOW, JESSIE GLASS, daughter of James Gow in Edinburgh, married Thomas Sinclair from Leith, in Valparaiso on 25 November 1870. [S#8583]

GOW, WILLIAM, Special Magistrate, late of Fort William, Inverness-shire, died in Honduras on 28 October 1838. [SG#8/737]

GRAHAM, BUCHANAN, son of Robert Graham MD Professor of Botany at Edinburgh University, died in Callao, Peru, on 29 March 1869. [S#8050]

GRAHAM, GEORGE TODHUNTER, born in 1839, died in Monte Video on 4 December 1875. [AO][S#10,130]

GRAHAM, JAMES, a merchant, married Harriett, daughter of James Cabot a merchant, in Mexico City 24 September 1846. [GM.NS.27.28]

GRAHAM, JOHN, born 4 July 1850, son of John Graham a surgeon [1821-1883] and Mary Anderson [died 1852], died in Vera Cruz 4 July 1871. [Girvan g/s, Ayrshire]

GRAHAM, WILLIAM, minister of St Andrew's, British Guiana, from 1840 to 18432, died in 1842. [F.7.676]

GRANT, ALEXANDER, at Plantation Good Intent, Demerara, 1810. [NAS.GD23.10.667]

GRANT, ALEXANDER, Mexico, married Marion Henderson Stirling, eldest daughter of Major W. Stirling, in Marseilles on 4 March 1853. [EEC#22406]

GRANT, ALPIN, in Woodly Park, Berbice, cnf 1867 Edinburgh. [NAS.SC70.1.137/586]

GRAHAM, J. ALFRED, MD, born 1819, died in Arequipa, Peru, on 10 April 1861. [S#1862]

GRAHAM, JAMES A., son of James Graham, Lynedoch Place, Glasgow, died in Buenos Ayres on 28 December 1867. [S#7656]

GRANT, CHARLES, from Banff, then in Argentina, cnf Edinburgh 1901. [NAS.SC70.1.406/943]

GRANT, DAVID STEWART RAMSAY, eldest son of Samuel Grant of Woodside, Brechin, Angus, married Jane Glegg, only daughter of Robert Glegg of HM Exchequer in Edinburgh, in Valparaiso,Chile, on 7 November 1877. [EC#29087]

GRANT, GEORGE, Captain of the <u>Acorn of Dundee</u>, died at Rio de Janeiro on 24 February 1873. [EC#27611]

GRANT, JOHN, in Demerara, died on 14 April 1837. Cnf Edinburgh 1838

GRANT, MARY JOANNA, only daughter of William Grant in Demerara, married Robert Tulloch, Golden Square, Edinburgh, during 1811. [SM#73.398]

GRANT, PETER, in British Guiana, 1835. [NAS.SC48.49.25.35/22]

GRANT, W.R., son of William Grant [1800-1890] and Mary Grant [1807-1891], settled in Buenos Ayres before 1889, died in Edinburgh during 1902. [Advie g/s]

GRAY, JOHN, eldest son of Thomas Gray in Duns, Berwickshire, died at the Rio Grande, South America, 1 October 1841. [EEC#20315]

GRAY, Reverend JOHN, in Valparaiso, cnf 1874 Edinburgh. [NAS.SC70.1.167/950]

GRAY, WILLIAM, eldest son of James and Christina Gray, 2 Broughton Place, Edinburgh, died in Rio de Janeiro on 12 April 1879. [S#11,184]

GRAY, WILLIAM, from Cosibrae, Cults, Aberdeenshire, died in Georgetown, Demerara, on 6 January 1881. [AJ:4.2.1897]

GREEN, JAMES, born in 1845, son of John Green a farmer in Percylaw, Clatt, died in Georgetown, Demerara, on 20 September 1864. [AJ:19.10.1864]

GRIERSON, JOSEPH, H.M. Consul in Chile, cnf Edinburgh 1894. [NAS.SC70.1.326/595]

GRIERSON, WILLIAM, born in 1825, died in Bella Vista, Entre Rios, on 27 December 1872. [AO]

GRIERSON, WILLIAM, born 1793, a farmer, with his wife Catherine, and three children, emigrated from Leith to Argentina on the Symmetry, master William Cochrane, on 22 May 1825. [SSP#18]

GRIEVE, THOMAS, born 1835, son of Thomas Grieve in Skelfhill, died in Valparaiso, Chile, on 2 June 1879. [S#11,414]

GUILD, JOHN, in Buenos Ayres, 1822, son of John Guild a merchant in Dundee. [NAS.CS17.1.42/34]

GUNN, Reverend AENEAS, born 1793, minister of St Luke's, British Guiana, 1825-1830, died 1830 in Demerara. [St Andrew's Scots Church g/s, Demerara][F.7.677]

GUTHRIE, STAIR, born 1843, son of George Guthrie of Appleby, Wigtonshire, an engineer and manager of the Chanaral Railway, died in Coquimba, Chile, on 22 November 1882. [S#12,328]

GUTHRIE, THOMAS, fourth son of Dr Guthrie, married Mary, youngest daughter of James Brown, in Quilmas, Buenos Ayres, on 24 May 1872. [S#9054]

HAIG, CECIL, born 1853, died in Tigre, Buenos Ayres, on 4 October 1877. [S#10,761]

HAIG, WILLIAM, minister of St Luke's, British Guiana, 1837, died 1837. [F.7.677]

HALDANE, ROBERT, the Mexican Consul, married Jane, daughter of Robert Kerr a surgeon in Portobello, in Carthagena on 24 June 1827. [BM#22.766]

HALDANE, ROBERT, possibly from Edinburgh, settled in Bogota before 1840. [NAS.SH]

HALDANE, ..., son of Robert Haldane, was born in Bogota on 4 September 1829. [S#1038.818]

HALDANE, ..., son of Robert Haldane, was born in Bogota on 4 November 1831. [GkAd#3820]

HALL, JAMES, in Santiago, Chile, cnf Edinburgh 1892. [NAS.SC70.1.310/386]

HALLIBURTON, GEORGE, in Buenos Ayres, died 25 June 1826. Cnf Edinburgh 1828. [NAS.PS3.15.81]

HALLIDAY, ALEXANDER, a merchant from Edinburgh, died at Port Mourant, Berbice, on 2 January 1840. [EEC#20027]

HALLIDAY, JAMES, with his wife, and children Margaret born 1815, Ann born 1817, William born 1820, Barbara born 1822, and Charles born 1825, emigrated from Cromarty on the Planet of London, Captain William Barclay, on 1 October 1825, landed at La Guayra on 2 December 1825, settled at Topo, Columbia, by 1827. [PRO.FO.18/47; FO.199/3/32]

HALLIDAY, JOHN, of Plantation Rosehall in Berbice, married Jessie Eliza Moon, youngest daughter of John Moon in Demerara, in Georgetown, Demerara, on 10 May 1872. [S#8988]

HALLIDAY, THOMAS SCOTT, born 1853, late of Bo'ness, West Lothian, died in Georgetown, Demerara, on 1 September 1881. [S#11,919]

HALLIDAY, WILLIAM, with his family, from Dumfries-shire, settled on the Rio Gallegos, Patagonia, in 1885. [SG.XLV.4/124]

HALLIDAY,........, was born at Plantation Windsor Forest, West Coast, Demerara, on 31 December 1873. [S#9521]

HALLIDAY,......., daughter of John Halliday, was born in Georgetown, Demerara, on 22 September 1878. [S#10,997]

HALLIDAY, ..., daughter of Thomas S. Halliday from Bo'ness, was born in Georgetown, Demerara, on 18 December 1879. [S#11,387]

HALLIDAY, ..., daughter of John Halliday, was born in Colonna House, Georgetown, Demerara, in 1881. [S#11,910]

HAMILTON, JAMES, British Vice Consul, died in Augustura, South America, on 7 July 1840. [W#71]

HAMILTON, Dr JAMES, a shipmaster and merchant at the Bay of Honduras, cnf 28 April 1803 Glasgow

HAMILTON, JOHN, factor at the Bay of Honduras for Hamilton, Gordon and Company, merchants in Edinburgh, 1800. [NAS.CS18.710.29]; cnf 13 May 1803 Glasgow. [NAS.CC9.7.75.588]

HAMILTON, JOHN JAMES, son of Reverend George Hamilton in Kirkcudbright, married Mary Amelia Susanna Foster, only daughter of John B. Foster, in Valparaiso 24 April 1862. [S#2182]

HAMILTON, JOHN SMART, late of Restalrig Terrace, Leith, then in Coatzacoalcos, Mexico, cnf Edinburgh 1900. [NAS.SC70.1.394/908]

HAMILTON, ROBERT, a merchant in Maricaibo, cnf 187 Edinburgh. [NAS.SC70.1.159/551]

HANNAH, ANDREW, CE, second son of William Hannah, Frederick Street, Edinburgh, married Rosa, eldest daughter of Edward Sennott, in Buenos Ayres on 6 December 1875. [S#10,145]

HARDIE, ROBERT, born in Hawick, Roxburghshire, on 20 October 1805, son of John Hardie a farmer, educated at Glasgow University, a minister in British Guina in 1837, died on 24 October 1837. [F.7.675]

HARDIE, ROBERT, an engineer, died in Surinam on 5 November 1861. [S#2030]

HARKNESS, THOMAS, born in 1821, an engineer, son of Thomas Harkness in Dumfries, died in Buenos Ayres on 21 May 1863. [AO]

HARPER, GEORGE, minister of St Clement's parish, British Guiana, 1857-1861. [F.7.676]

HARPER, WILLIAM, educated at St Andrews University, minister of St James, British Guiana, 1868, died 8 August 1887. [F.7.677]

HARRISON, CHARLES, born 1827, died 1861 in Demerara. [St Andrew's Scots Church g/s, Demerara]

HARRISON, FRANCIS H., from Glasgow, a merchant in Rio de Janeiro, 23 August 1898. [NAS.SC70.6]

HARRISON, ..., son of Francis Henry Harrison, was born in Rio de Janeiro on 11 March 1878. [EC#29191]

HARROW, MAGGIE, wife of William Goodfellow, Estancia de la Macedonia, died in Tindal, Buenos Ayres, on 12 May 1874. [EC#28002][S#9660]

HART, JOHN, from Glasgow, died in Valparaiso on 24 February 1849. [SG#18/1817]

HARTHILL, ADAM, in Berbice, married Mary Dear Bowne, youngest daughter of John T. B. Bowne of Bellfield, Barbados, in Barbados on 28 November 1854. [EEC#22681]

HARVEY, JOHN, in Payta, Peru, cnf 1868 Edinburgh. [NAS.SC70.1.141/1]

HASTIE, ARCHIBALD, in Azul, Buenos Ayres, son of Archibald Hastie, a baker in Paisley, and his wife Margaret MacFarlane who died 26 September 1880. [NAS.SH.10.10.1885]

HAY, DAVID, of the Customs, died in Surinam on 30 October 1807. [SM#67.399]

HENDERSON, JAMES, of Harrop and Henderson, in Para, Brazil, 1832. [NAS.GD76.454]

HENDERSON, JAMES, from Edinburgh, died in Buenos Ayres 3 December 1871. [S#8861]

HENDERSON, JOHN, born in 1840, died in Arica, Peru, on 2 April 1876. [EC#28601]

HENDERSON, JOHN, of the Bank of London, Mexico and South America, sometime of the Bank of Scotland in Edinburgh, died in Mexico on 20 August 1883, son of John Henderson, West Port, Brechin, Angus. [S#12,518]

HENDERSON, MARGARET WEMYSS, and ELLEN ANN, twin daughters of James Henderson, a merchant, and Catherine Black, were born in Valparaiso on 22 June 1823 and baptised 10 May 1825. [St Peter's Episcopal Church Records, Kirkcaldy]

HENDERSON, ROBERT, a blacksmith, born 1825, son of .... Henderson of Raith, died in Barracas al Sud, Buenos Ayres, on 28 February 1887. [FFP]

HENDERSON, SARAH WARDILOVE, born 1811 second daughter of James Henderson, HM Consul General, died in Bogota, Columbia, on 12 January 1825. [S#533.112]

HENDERSON, Reverend THOMAS, '49 years a missionary', died in New Amsterdam, Berbice, 30 July 1870. [S#8449][F.7.673]

HENDERSON, ..., son of James Henderson, HM Consul General in Columbia, born in Bogota on 8 February 1830. [PA#40]

HENDERSON,...., daughter of James Henderson the HM Consul General for Columbia, was born in Bogota on 10 June 1826. [BM#20.919]

HENDERSON,...., daughter of James Henderson the HM Consul General for Columbia, was born in Bogota on 18 September 1827. [BM#23.661]

HENDERSON, Mrs...., wife of James Henderson HM Consul General for Columbia, died in Bogota on 18 September 1827. [EA#6700.103]

HENDERSON, WILLIAM, son of Dr Henderson a physician in Dundee, died in Quito during November 1822. [BM#14.624]

HENDERSON, ..., daughter of William R. Henderson, was born in Valparaiso on 7 February 1876. [EC#28552][S#10,206]

HENDERSON, ..., daughter of W. R. Henderson, was born in Valparaiso, Chile, on 19 January 1884. [S#12,688]

HENDRIE, GEORGE, born in 1856, son of George Hendrie, farmer in Craig, [1814-1867] and Jane Skinner [1826-1860] Straiton, Ayrshire, died in Rio de Janeiro on 15 November 1875. [EC#28460][Straiton g/s]

HENRY, JOHN FRENCH, born in 1840, of Horrock, henry and Company, merchants in Rio Grande du Sol, Brazil, died in Rio de Janeiro, on 16 November 1873. [EC#277852]

HENRY, WILLIAM, a Colonel in the service of the Republic of Columbia, died in Carthagena on his way to Bogota during 1826. [EA]

HERON, WILLIAM, died in the British Hospital, Buenos Ayres, on 6 February 1899. [Mochrum g/s, Wigtownshire]

HEYWORTH, ..., daughter of Frederick Heyworth, was born at Estancia Aji, Lucas Gonzales, Entre Rios, Argentine, on 8 January 1899. [S#17358]

HIGGINS, SAMUEL G., born in 1872, son of James E. Higgins and Margaret Goodwin, died in Rio de Janeiro on 2 March 1894. [Mochrum g/s, Wigtownshire]

HILL, WALTER HOWETSON, in Valparaiso, cnf 1872 Edinburgh. [NAS.SC70.1.159/418]

HODGE, JOHN, from Crail, Fife, died in Belize, Honduras, in 1869. [EFR.21.5.1869]

HOME, JAMES, at the Great Black River, Mosquito Shore, 1778. [NAS.RS27.237.24]

HONEYMAN, ISABELLA WALLACE only daughter of Thomas Honeyman, Veitch Park, Haddington, East Lothian, married James MacFadyen of the National Bank of Chile, at 233 Calle de Victoria, Valparaiso, in 1869. [S#8087]

HOOD, JANET, daughter of William Hood in Strathvithie Mains, St Andrews, Fife, married John Orr Love, in Demerara on 11 December 1885. [FH]

HOOD, JOHN, born 1861, eldest son of William Hood, Strathvithie Mains, St Andrews, Fife, drowned in Abary Creek, Demerara, on 2 March 1896. [FH]

HOOD, ROBERT RAEBURN, manager of the Aranco Coal Company in Coronel, Chile, around 1891. [NAS.SH.26.10.1891]

HOOD, THOMAS, formerly manager of Seafield Farm, St Andrews, Fife, died in Demerara on 10 June 1833. [FH]

HOPE, Dr JOHN, died in Demerara 12 August 1804. [West Linton g/s, Peebles-shire]

HOPE, ..., son of D. Hope, was born at Mouro Velho, Brazil, on 18 May 1855. [EEC#22763]

HOPE, Dr GEORGE C., married Maria, eldest daughter of Dr Thomas Walker of Polmont Bank, Stirlingshire, in Morro Velho, Brazil, on 20 May 1854. [EEC#22610]

HOPE, JAMES, son of Alexander Hope in Glasgow, died in Mexillomes on 15 August 1875. [EC#28397]

HOPE, WILLIAM, Los Amigos, Rosario, Argentina, married Kate C. Grant, Parana, in Los Alamos on 12 September 1883. [S#12,575]

HORDEN, G. W., of Eyhumbogo, died in Ayro, Chile, on 26 March 1877. [S#10,544]

HORN, JAMES BREMNER, born 1851, son of Robert Horn, a grocer in Largo, Fife, died in Mejillones, Bolivia, on 14 October 1877. [FH][S#10,737]

HOUSTOUN, JAMES, in Carthagena 16 August 1730. [BMu.Sloane #4051/85]

HOWDEN, MARION, second daughter of John Howden in Nether Braco, Perthshire, married William Balgonie a merchant, at Windsar Villa, Georgetown, Demerara, 15 November 1870. [S#8545]

HOWELL, ALEXANDER RUTHERFORD, MA, a minister in Buenos Ayres from 1895 to 1897. [F#7.682]

HUIE, JAMES, son of James Huie and Margaret Haldane, died in Costa Rica 16 March 1893. [East Preston Street cemetery, Edinburgh]

HUME, HENRIETTA, daughter of Mr Hume land surveyor in Belize, married Alexander Williamson in Belize on 6 August 1868. [S#7847]

HUMPHREYS, WILLIAM, born 1814, Sheriff of Essequibo, died at Bellfield House, Essequibo, on 11 May 1877. [S#10,578]

HUNTER, ROBERT, born 1839, died in Buenos Ayres in 1871. [SRP#365]

HUNTER, WILLIAM, from Townhead, Monaive, Dumfries-shire, died in Concordia on 15 May 1872. [S#9046]

HUNTER, ..., daughter of J. D. Hunter, died in Arequipa, Peru, 21 July 1871. [S#8766]

HUNTER, WILLIAM, a farmer in Concordia, South America, cnf 1873 Edinburgh. [NAS.SC70.1.163/5]

HUNTLY, ..., daughter of Reverend B. C. Huntly, was born in Sao Paulo, Brazil, on 6 July 1877. [EC#28975]

HUNTER, CHARLES, Captain of the Royal Artillery, in Demerara, died 24 June 1856. Cnf 1856 Edinburgh [NAS.CC8.8.inv.1856]

HUNTER, Dr JACOB D., in Arequira, Peru, 8 June 1888. [NAS.RS.Edinburgh.162/47]

HUNTER, JOHN, born 1821, eldest son of Alexander Hunter, Writer to the Signet, died in Buenos Ayres on 17 December 1868. [S#7727]

HUNTER, WILLIAM HUMPHREY, jr., eldest son of Mr Hunter a merchant in Greenock, died in Demerara during 1813. [EA#5174.13]

HUSKIE, JAMES, born in Larbert 26 February 1826, son of James Huskie and Elizabeth Gillon, educated at Edinburgh

University, minister of St Saviour's British Guiana 1861-1884. [F.7.679]

HUTCHEON, D., born 1773, a militaary surgeon in Berbice, died there on 7 March 1809. [SM#71.398]

HUTCHISON, ANDREW, born in 1786, son of Andrew Hutchison and Mary Malcolm, surgeon on HMS Sapphire, died in Chargre on the Spanish Main, on 17 September 1819. [Burntisland g/s, Fife]

HUTCHISON, JAMES, merchant at the Bay of Honduras, died 179-. [NAS.CC8.8.130-2]

HUTCHISON, WILLIAM, born 1837, a farmer, died in Buenos Ayres 6 June 1870. [S#8418]

HUTSON, JOHN RICH FARRE, born 1797, eldest son of Henry Hutson a physician in Demerara, educated at Glasgow University in 1816, graduated MD in 1817, a physician in Demerara, died on 13 October 1864. [MAGU#293]

HUTTON, JAMES, engineer on the SS Rio de Janeiro, son of John Hutton (1798-1871) and Euphemia Dunn (1825-1875) of 48 Clerk Street, Edinburgh, died in Rio de Janeiro on 16 March 1876. [East Preston Street cemetery, Edinburgh] [S#10,218]

HYDE, JAMES, and his wife Susan Campbell, a merchant from Greenock, a woodcutter in Honduras 1814, 1820, 1822. [NAS.RD5.63.5; RD5.177.225; CS17.1.42/63]

HYSLOP, ADAM, in La Serena, from Moffat, Dumfries-shire, married Havilah Sarah Thomas, eldest daughter of Mauris Thomas from Cornwall, in La Pampa Alta, La Serena, Chile, on 23 June 1873. [S#9418]

IMLACH, ROBERT WRIGHT, Crown Solicitor of British Guiana, cnf Edinburgh 1889. [NAS.SC70.1.274/745]

INGLIS, GEORGE, a planter in Demerara in 1795, [NAS.GD23.5.352]; from Demerara, married Helen Alves, daughter of Dr John Alves a physician in Inverness, in Springfield on 24 July 1798. [SM#60.575]

INGLES AND HALL, cotton merchants in Glasgow and Demerara, around 1825. [NAS.CS96.378]

INGRAM, ISAAC, in Antigua, Guatamala, cnf 1874 Edinburgh. [NAS.SC70.1.168/600]

INGRAM, JAMES, Santiago de Chili, died 2 June 1847. Cnf 1848 Edinburgh

INGRAM, WILLIAM, son of James Ingram in Wester Dalwick, died in Venezuela on 4 June 1883. [S#12,498]

INNES, WILLIAM in Elgin, Morayshire, late of Berbice, 18 June 1850. [NAS.RGS#245/57/135]

IRVINE, HUGH, in Berbice, then in Glasgow, cnf 6 February 1810 Glasgow. [NAS.CC9.7.77.118]

IRVING, WILLIAM PAGAN, an engineer in Rosario de Santa Fe, South America, cnf Edinburgh 1887. [NAS.SC70.1.256/584]

IVOL, CHARLES CAMPBELL, in Valparaiso, cnf Edinburgh 1898. [NAS.SC70.1.367/78]

IVOL, ..., daughter of James Ivol an engineer from Glasgow, was born in Valparaiso on 29 October 1875. [EC#28467]

JACK, GEORGE JOHN, born 1853, youngest son of John Jack in East Mains, Lauder, died in Georgetown, Demerara, on 3 January 1881. [S#12,029]

JACKSON, ANDREW, Georgetown, Demerara, died 5 June 1835, inv. 1840 Edinburgh

JACKSON,...., son of Reverend John Jackson, was born in Belize, British Honduras, on 25 December 1877. [S#10,793]

JACKSON, ..., son of Reverend John Jackson, was born in Belize, British Honduras, on 25 August 1883. [S#12,542]

JAFFREY, ROBERT, an engineer in Brazil, cnf 1867 Edinburgh. [NAS.SC70.1.136/30]

JAMIESON, JAMES, a merchant in Demerara 1811. [NAS.RD5.88.666]; died in Demerara during 1818. [S#51.18]

JAMIESON, JAMES FERGUSON, a merchant in Trinidad and Demerara, cnf 1868 Edinburgh. [NAS.SC70.1.140/505]

JAMIESON, THOMAS, a surgeon in Guayaquil, South America, son of William Jamieson and Elizabeth Jane Turnbull in Portobello, Edinburgh, 1851. [NAS.SH]

JAMIESON, WILLIAM, MD, born in Edinburgh, a Caballero of Spain, late Professor of Botany and Chemistry at Quito University, Director of the Mint of Ecuador, died in Quito on 23 June 1873. [S#9385]

JARDINE, CHARLES K., married Bridget Semple, eldest daughter of David Semple a merchant in Glasgow, in Georgetown, Demerara, on 11 February 1875. [EC#28224]

JARDINE, FRANCIS, minister of St Saviour's, British Guiana, 1862-1878, returned to Scotland. [F.7.680]

JEFFREY, MAGGIE, late of North Queensferry, Fife, wife of Robert Penny superintendent of the Railway Works at Chomillos, Peru, died there on 11 April 1873. [FA][S#9303]

JEFFREY, Mrs, wife of Alexander Jeffrey late shepherd in East Lothian, died in Paysandu, South America, on 29 August 1884. [S#12892]

JOBSON, RACHEL SCOTT, eldest daughter of David Jobson a solicitor in Dundee, married John Gentle in Belize, Honduras, 16 November 1861. [S#2055]

JOHNSTON, FRANCIS, a surgeon, son of Reverend Andrew Johnston in Salton, died on the Plantation Lusiqual, Demerara, 28 July 1830. [S#1121]

JOHNSTON, GEORGE RICHARDSON, born in 1848, eldest son of James Charles Johnston, Commander of the Royal Navy, Edinburgh, died in Camps of Santa Fe, on 30 December 1873. [EC#27899][S#9539]

JOHNSTON, GEORGE, jr., in New Orleans, cnf Edinburgh 1901. [NAS.SC70.1.408/391]

JOHNSTON, GEORGINA, younger daughter of George Johnston of HM Customs in Aberdeen, wife of Dr Hoskins, died in Ascuncion, Paraguay, on 3 July 1890. [AJ:3.9.1890]

JOHNSTON, JAMES THOMSON, son of Adam Thomson, tenant in Millknow, Glasgow, died in Demerara 1853. [S.14.1.1854]

JOHNSTON, JOHN, MD, born 1812, eldest son of Alexander Johnston, died in Asuncion, South America, on 9 October 1857. [Edinburgh, St Cuthbert's g/s]

JOHNSTON, Dr RICHARD, son of William Johnston in Lockerbie, Dumfries-shire, died in Coldera, Chile, on 11 August 1866. [AO]

JOHNSTON, ROBERT ANTHONY, born 1847, son of George Johnston of Bristol and grandson of Richard Johnston of Caldwellpath, died in Georgetown, Demerara, on 26 July 1886. [AO:5.11.1886]

JOHNSTON, RODERICK, a planter at Plantation Aurora, St John's, Essequibo, died 20 March 1852. Cnf Edinburgh 1853

JOHNSTON, SAMUEL POWER, born 1814, of Pernambuco, died in Wood Hey, Rock Ferry, Cheshire, on 15 February 1881. [S#11,731]

JOHNSTON, SAMUEL, born 1859, only son of S. P. Johnston late of Cheshire and Pernambuco, died in Pernambuco on 2 January 1884. [S#12,661]

JOHNSTONE, SARAH, daughter of Dr J. M. Johnstone late Health Officer of Demerara, married J. H. Dodd, government surveyor, in Kingston, Jamaica, on 24 July 1876. [S#10,318]

JOHNSTON, THOMAS, born 1840, youngest son of William Johnston of Middlerigg, Polmont, Stirlingshire, died in San Luis, Peru, on 26 November 1879. [S#11,380]

JOHNSTON, WALTER, son of Mr Johnston, 233 West Regent Street, Glasgow, died in Nueva de Julio, Buenos Ayres, on 16 August 1882. [S#12,235]

JOHNSTON, WILLIAM, of Seafield, late in Demerara, 21 October 1821. [NAS.RS.Annan#3/88]

JOHNSTON, WILLIAM, a surgeon, died in Demerara on 11 March 1829. [BM#26.268]

JOHNSTON, ..., daughter of Powell Ruxton Johnston, was born in San Jose, Monte Video, on 16 June 1874. [EC#28027][S#9679]

JOLLY, DAVID L., Real de Monte, son of David L. Jolly a banker in Perth, married Margaret Elizabeth Stewart MacGregor, youngest daughter of Robert MacGregor, Campbelltown, Argyll, in the British Consulate in Mexico on 2 April 1860. [DC#23504][W#21/2196][S#1538]

JOLLY, DAVID LEITCH, born 1833, accidentally killed in Tampico, Mexico, on 10 December 1882. [S#12,300]

JOLLY, ROBERT KEITH, fourth son of William Gairdner Jolly, died in Tampico on 30 May 1867. [S#7484]

JOLLY, ..., daughter of David L. Jolly jr., was born in Tampico, Mexico, on 2 November 1873. [S#9449]

JORIE, ALEXANDER, born in 1801, son of John Jorie {1753-1813} a merchant in Whithorn, Wigtownshire, and Mary Allan {1770-1850}, died in Demerara on 1 August 1819. [Whithorn g/s]

JUNOR, MARY WYLLIE, daughter of Hugh Junor, New Mill, Strichen, Aberdeenshire, married Thomas Woodman, Plantation Adelphi, Berbice, in Georgetown, Demerara, on 3 September 1878. [S#10,984]

JUNOR, MARY WYLLIE, wife of Thomas Woodman, died at Plantation Adelphi, Berbice, on 4 February 1880. [S#11,430]

KALLEY, ROBERT REID, MD, born 8 September 1809, a teacher and pastor in Rio de Janeiro and in Pernambuco, Brazil, from 1855 to 1888, died 17 January 1888. [Dean g/s, Edinburgh]

KEAY, DAVID, born in 1816 son of William Keay and Ann Soutar, died in Mexico during August 1865. [Lethendy g/s, Perthshire]

KEIR, WILLIAM AUGUSTUS, only son of Patrick S.Keir of Kildrogan, died in Valparaiso on 15 February 1879. [S#11141]

KELLIE, JOHN, in Chasromus, Argentina, cnf Edinburgh 1897. [NAS.SC70.1.362/132]

KELLOCK, GEORGE, born 1800, special magistrate, eldest son of Alexander Kellock MD in Berwick-on-Tweed, died in Leguan, Demerara, 12 January 1839. [EEC#19872]

KEMLO, Dr WILLIAM, of the 70th Regiment, died in Berbice on 10 March 1840, inv. 1841 Edinburgh

KEMP, WILLIAM FINNIE, eldest son of James Kemp in Edinburgh, married Isobel Matson, youngest daughter of Charles Matson of Rio de Janeiro, there on 10 May 1877. [S#10,555]

KENNEDY, ALEXANDER, a merchant in Chanaral, Chile, second son of Daniel Kennedy in Edinburgh, married Jane Peebles, second daughter of Robert Peebles of Chanaral, in Valparaiso on 22 November 1877. [S#10,762]

KENNEDY, DONALD, emigrated from Cromarty on the <u>Planet of London</u>, Captain William Barclay, on 1 October 1825, landed at La Guayra on 2 December 1825, settled at Topo, Columbia, finally settled in Caracas as a merchant, married Amanda Maria Hahn.

KENNEDY, DUNCAN, emigrated from Cromarty on the <u>Planet of London</u>, Captain William Barclay, on 1 October 1825, landed at La Guayra on 2 December 1825, settled at Topo, Columbia, later moved to Caracas, finally settled in Aroa as accountant of the Bolivar Mining Association, murdered there on 8 August 1836

KENNEDY, EWAN, youngest son of Daniel Kennedy a livestock agent in Edinburgh, died in Chanaral, Chile, on 12 October 1879. [S#11,352]

KENNEDY, EWEN, born 1880, only son of Donald Kennedy [1846-1918] and Annie Brown [1852-1942], died in Inique, Chile, on 23 May 1909. [Dean g/s, Edinburgh]

KENNEDY, HUGH, with his wife and family, emigrated from Cromarty on the Planet of London, Captain William Barclay, on 1 October 1825, landed at La Guayra on 2 December 1825, settled at Topo, Columbia, later moved to Caracas, finally settled in Guelph, Canada, in 1827.

KENNEDY, JAMES LENOX, born in Kirkcudbright, son of Captain John Kennedy and Mary Lenox, emigrated via Lisbon to New York on the Glenthorn in September 1815, a merchant in New York and in Mazatlan, Mexico, US Consul there, died in Vera Cruz, Mexico, on 6 January 1867. [ANY.2.83]

KENNEDY, JOHN, with his wife, and children Hugh born 1813, Margaret born 1815, Elizabeth born 1817, Mary born 1819, Simon born 1821, and John born 1826, emigrated from Cromarty on the Planet of London, Captain William Barclay, on 1 October 1825, landed at La Guayra on 2 December 1825, settled at Topo, Columbia, by 1827. [PRO.FO.18/47; FO.199/3/32]

KENNEDY, OWEN, with his wife, and children Margaret born 1821, Mary born 1823, emigrated from Cromarty on the Planet of London, Captain William Barclay, on 1 October 1825, landed at La Guayra on 2 December 1825, settled at Topo, Columbia, by 1827. [PRO.FO.18/47; FO.199/3/32]

KENNEDY, WALTER, son of Reverend Hugh Kennedy and Margaret Scott in Cavers, Roxburghshire, a planter in Surinam, died in London during 1777. [F.2.106]

KENNOWAY, WILLIAM THOMSON, died in San Jose, Costa Rica, on 1 February 1880. [FH]

KERR, JANE, daughter of Robert Kerr a surgeon in Portobello, married Robert Haldane, the Mexican consul, in Carthagena on 24 July 1827. [BM#22.766]

KERR, JOHN, late of Corunna Plce, Bonnington Road, Leith, died in St Louis, South America, 2 January 1873. [S#9202]

KERR, SIMON, of the English Academy in Coquimba, South America, married Christina Campbell, youngest daughter of D. Campbell in Leith, in Coquimba on 30 March 1861. [S#1842]; in Serena, Chile, cnf 1876 Edinburgh. [NAS.SC70.1.177/10]

KERR, WILLIAM, born 1840, from 80 South Clerk Street, Edinburgh, died at Minas Schweger, Coronel, Chile, on 18 October 1883. [S#12,610]

KERR, ..., son of Simon Kerr, was born in Ballinar, Chile, on 2 April 1862. [S#2171]

KERR, ..., son of Simon Kerr, was born in Serena, Coquimbo, Chile, on 23 December 1870. [S#8608]

KEITH, PATRICK, eldest son of Reverend Keith in Golspie, died in Berbice on 10 August 1805. [SM#68.78]

KELTIE, JOHN, only son of Robert Keltie in Demerara, died in London on 30 November 1819. [BM#6.360]

KETCHEN, DAVID, late chief officer of the Chilean brig <u>Challenger</u> and eldest son of Robert Ketchen in Pittenweem, Fife, died aboard thee <u>Jane Innes of Glasgow</u> in the Pacific Ocean 1 October 1851. [PR.31.1.1852]

KIDD, JOHN, married Elizabeth S. Trilia, at George McLean's residence Calle Paraguay 133, Buenos Ayres, 8 November 1873. [S#9484]

KIDD, ..., daughter of John H. Kidd, was born at Calle Belle Nista, Buenos Ayres, on 23 July 1876. [S#10,327]

KING, JAMES, born 1830, son of James King and Mary Tassie in Paisley, Renfrewshire, died in Chile 1870. [Paisley Abbey g/s]

KING, JOHN, born 1833, son of James King and Isabella Sharp, died in Rio de Janeiro on 22 June 1850. [Perth, Greyfriars, g/s]

KING, WILLIAM H., son of George King in Glasgow, died on Plantation Greenfield, Demerara, on 10 March 1839. [SG#8/769]

KINGSTON, JOHN, Clairmont, Demerara, married Louisa Henrietta, second daughter of Sir Charles Edmonstone of Duntreath, Stirlingshire, in Hampton on 15 December 1829. [BM#27.549]

KINNEAR, MAGGIE, daughter of John Kinnear, a baker in Links Street, Kirkcaldy, wife of James Davidson an engineer, died in Savanna, San Jose, Costa Rica, on 2 July 1888. [FFP]

KINNISON, JOHN, minister in British Guiana around 1860. [F.7.678]

KIRKE, ROBERT, born in 1816, son of Robert Kirke and Helen Balfour, Greenmount, Burntisland, Fife, and Waterloo Nickery, Surinam, died on 3 January 1894. [Cairneyhill g/s, Fife]

KIRKWOOD, JAMES, eldest son of Reverend T. D.Kirkwood in Dunbernie, married Maria Raquel Novillo, eldest daughter of Andres S. Novillo, of Cordova, Argentina, in Tacna, Peru, on 11 August 1877. [S#10,670]

KIRKWOOD, ..., daughter of James Kirkwood, was born in Tacna, Arica, Peru, on 3 June 1878. [EC#29290][S#10,942]

KIRKWOOD, ..., daughter of James Kirkwood, was born in Tacna, Peru, on 16 December 1880. [S#11,474]

KIRKPATRICK, Sir CHARLES SHARPE, died in Libertad, Central America, on 9 November 1867. [S#7591]

KNIGHT, ADAM, from Portsoy, Banffshire, died in Demerara during 1808. [SM#70.477]

KNIGHT, DAVID, born in Arbroath, Angus, during 1799, died in Georgetown, Demerara, on 23 November 1831. [AJ#4387]

KYLE, JOHN, born in 1820, son of James Kyle, died in Berbice on 26 December 1845. [Chapel Yard g/s, Inverness]

LAIDLAW, THOMAS, from Glasgow, died in Valparaiso on 22 July 1882. [S#12,228]

LAING, HENRY, born in 1863, youngest son of A. R. Laing of Glasterlaw, died in Pernambuco, Brazil, on 26 February 1877. [EC#28854]

LAMB, WILLIAM, born in 1825, eldest son of Mr Primrose Lamb an agent in Ayr, died in Demerara on 22 December 1838. [SG#8/746]

LAMBERT, ..., son of Charles S. Lambert, was born in Copiapo, Chile, during 1826. [BM#21.771]

LANDALE, HENRY, an engineer from Leven, Fife, husband of Christine Forbes, died in Campos, Brazil, on 24 August 1887.[FFP]

LANDALE, ..., daughter of Henry Landale an engineer from Kirkcaldy, was born at Capivary Central Sugar Factory, Brazil, on 7 February 1885. [FFP]

LANG, JOHN WILLIAM, born 1835, son of William Lang and Isabella Murray, a surgeon in Mexico, died in Southampton 18 February 1865. [Edinburgh, St Cuthbert's g/s]

LARNACH, WILLIAM, born in 1831, son of William Larnach and Barbara McDonald, died in Buenos Ayres on 2 January 1864, buried in the British Cemetery. [Watten g/s, Caithness]

LATHAM, ANITA LORETTA, younger daughter of Wilfred Latham, Los Alamos, Buenos Ayres, married William Kemmis, Los Rosas, Buenos Ayres, in Duns, Berwickshire, on 28 October 1876. [S#10,385]

LAURENT, AMIDIE, a merchant in Belize, cnf 1873 Edinburgh. [NAS.SC70.1.161/773]

LAURIE, Colonel JOHN, born 1720, son of Reverend James Laurie, [died 1764] and Ann Ord, [died 1747], in Kilmichael, Ayrshire, Governor of the Mosquito Shore, died in Glasgow on 20 December 1800. [F#3.45][GM.70.1298]

LAW, ALEXANDER, born around 1782, son of James Law in Glasgow, died in Demerara during July 1802. [EA#4040.02]

LAW, WILLIAM, born during 1830 son of John and Mary Law, died in Rio de Janeiro during 1852. [Crail g/s, Fife]

LAW, Dr WILLIAM, from Roadhead, Lochwinnoch, Renfrewshire, died in Belize on 2 May 1878. [EC#29229]; cnf 1879 Edinburgh. [NAS.SC70.1.192/145]

LAW, WILLIAM, born 1853, son of William Law (1827-1890) forester in Bowland, Roxburghshire, and Ann Robinson (1830-1901), died in Sao Paulo, Brazil, 24 August 1887. [Lilliesleaf g/s, Roxburghshire]

LAWRIE, JAMES GORDON, in Buenos Ayres, 5 January 1886. [NAS.RS.Edinburgh.155/40]; cnf Edinburgh 1896. [NAS.SC70.1.351/24]

LAWRIE, JAMES, a merchant, Poyais County, Mosquito Shore, 1772, 1774. [NAS.GD77.165][NLS.ms3942/173]

LAWRIE, ..., daughter of Dr Lawrie, was born in Monte Video on 6 May 1867. [S#7456]

LAWSON, JAMES, an engineer, son of Robert Lawson in South Vennel, Fisherrow, Musselburgh, died in Cera, Brazil, on 21 March 1874. [S#9687]

LAWSON, ROBERT J., only son of John Lawson a merchant in Dumfries, died in Maracaibo on 1 August 1822. [BM#12.69]

LAWSON, WALTER SCOTT, died in Belize, British Honduras, on 4 February 1879. [S#11,129]

LEDINGHAM, WILLIAM, son of William Ledingham and Margaret Bartlett, a merchant in Buenos Ayres, died there during 1871. [Dyce g/s, Aberdeenshire]

LEES, ..., daughter of Thomas Murray Lees, accountant of theLondon and River Plate Bank, was born in Paysandu, South America, on 8 February 1899. [S#17,379]

LEGGAT, JAMES, in Buenos Ayres, cnf 1871 Edinburgh. [NAS.SC70.1.155/628]

LEIGHTON, ALEXANDER, in Estancia Santa Kilda, Uruguay, cnf 1899 Edinburgh. [NAS.SC70.1.385/217]

LEIGHTON, DAVID, a merchant from Bruntsfield Place, Edinburgh, died in Santa Kilda, Banda Oriental, cnf Edinburgh 1891. [NAS.SC70.1.299/504]

LEIGHTON, Dr THOMAS, eldest son of Alexander Leighton in Dundee, died in Valparaiso, Chile, on 18 April 1837. [AJ#4697]

LEIGHTON, ..., daughter of David Leighton, was born in Buenos Ayres on 26 February 1899. [S#17,373]

LEISHMAN, GEORGE, fifth son of James Leishman, Broomrigge, Dollar, Clackmannanshire, died in Chascomus, Buenos Ayres, in November 1875. [S#10,108]

LESLIE, JAMES WALKER, born 1849, son of John Leslie a surgeon in Inverurie, Aberdeenshire, died on Plantation Bel-Air, Demerara, on 30 September 1872. [AJ: 6.11.1872]

LESLIE, ..., daughter of George Leslie, was born in Paramaribo, Surinam, 25 December 1861. [S#2066]

LESLIE, LOUISA ANN, infant daughter of George Leslie, died in Paramaribo, Surinam, on 27 January 1863. [S#2406]

LESSELS, ANDREW, born 1829, fifth son of George Lessels and Martha Henderson in Newburgh, Fife, died in Panama on 27 August 1868. [Fife Herald][Newburgh g/s]

LEVEN, JAMES, born 1829, son of John Leven an Excise Collector, died 9 March 1850 in Maccio, Brazil. [Canongate g/s, Edinburgh]

LEYS, ROBERT, married Euphemia M. Greig, only daughter of John Greig of Buenos Ayres, there on 25 April 1845. [Banner#6/298]

LEYS, ROBERT, born 1800, died in Buenos Ayres on 28 September 1850. [AJ#5374]

LIDDAL, THOMAS YOUNG, a merchant in Belize, died 2 September 1844. Cnf Edinburgh 1850

LIDDELL, ALEXANDER, born 1858, eldest son of Thomas Liddell, 161 West Fountainbridge, Edinburgh, died in Havanna,Cuba, on 17 August 1878. [S#10,967]

LILLIE, GEORGE, formerly a member of the Legislative Council of British Guiana, died in Georgetown, Demerara, on 26 January 1874. [S#9538]

LILLIE, GORDON, minister of St Mary's, British Guiana, 1861-1874. [F.7.679]

LILLIE, ..., daughter of David W. Lillie, was born in Berbice on 10 February 1863. [S#2419]

LINDSAY, JAMES, of Gualaguayehu, son of William Lindsay, Stanhope, Peebles-shire, died at the residence of R. Runciman in Buenos Ayres on 24 April 1877, cnf 1878 Edinburgh. [NAS.SC70.1.189/185][S#10,563]

LINDSAY, P., in Demerara, 1798. [EUL.ms#Dc4.41.146]

LINDSAY, WALLACE, FRCPE, born 30 May 1837, son of James Lindsay [1804-1874] and Helen Baird Lauder [1804-1883], assistant surgeon of the 30th Regiment, died at Cordsal, British Honduras, on 31 December 1862. [Dean g/s, Edinburgh] [S#2405]

LINN, THOMAS G., son of Robert Linn in Biggar, Lanarkshire, died on Plantation La Belle Alliance, Essequibo, British Guina, 7 October 1871. [S#8817]

LITTLE, JOHN, in Bahia, Brazil, graduated MD from King's College, Aberdeen, on 18 December 1824. [AUL]

LIVINGSTONE, JOHN, son of Samuel Livingstone a merchant in Greenock, died in Demerara on 9 May 1848. [SG#17/1735]

LIZARS, WILLIAM, in Georgetown, British Guina, son of William Lizars, a shoemaker in Leith, 1833. [NAS.SH]

LIZARS, WILLIAM HORNE, in Buenos Ayres, cnf Edinburgh 1888. [NAS.SC70.1.266/285]

LOCH, GRANVILLE G., in Niceragua 1847-1851. [NAS.GD268/47]

LOCKHART, WILLIAM, a cabinet maker in Monte Video, 1853. [NAS.SC48.49.25.54/6]

LOCHORE, ..., daughter of H. W.Lochore, was born in Belgrano, Buenos Ayres, on 18 March 1884. [S#12,726]

LOGAN, ANDREW, MD, born 10 January 1799, settled in Demerara, died on 23 October 1888. [Sorn g/s, Ayrshire]

LOGAN, JOHN W., second son of John Logan of Eastshield, Carnwath, Lanarkshire, died on the voyage home from Buenos Ayres on 9 August 1867. [S#7518]

LORIMER, JANET, or CHALMERS, in British Guina, 17 May 1879. [NAS.RS.Edinburgh.135/110]

LORIMER, ..., daughter of Robert Scott Lorimer, Plantation Wales, Demerara, was born in Cheltenham, England, on 11 January 1876.[EC#28482]

LOUDON, JOHN, MD, in Pernambuco, died 23 May 1843, cnf Edinburgh 1843

LOUSON, JAMES, born 1809, son of John Louson, 1784-1829, a merchant in Arbroath, and his wife Ann C Stevenson, 1785-1830, died in Para, South America, 27 February 1833. [Arbroath Abbey g/s]

LOVE, JOHN, with his wife and daughter Elizabeth born 1825, emigrated from Cromarty on the Planet of London, Captain William Barclay, on 1 October 1825, landed at La Guayra on 2 December 1825, settled at Topo, Columbia, by 1827. [PRO.FO.18/47; FO.199/3/32]

LOW, ALEXANDER FAIRWEATHER, son of James Low (died 1819) and Ann Fairweather (died 1858), a merchant in Mexico. [Constitution Road g/s, Dundee]

LOW, WILLIAM, a merchant, died in Berbice on 8 June 1802. [EA#4054.02][GkAd#88]

LOWSON, JAMES, born 1809, eldest son of John Lowson, a merchant, and Ann O. Stevenson in Arbroath, Angus, died in Para 27 February 1823. [Arbroath Abbey g/s]

LYELL, ANDREW ALEXANDER, died in Mexico on 12 January 1846. [AJ#5122]

LYELL, JAMES, in Mexico, married Eliza, daughter of Captain Martyn of the 11TH Foot, on 10 July 1838. [AJ#4722]

LYELL, JOHN THOMAS STUART, a surgeon, eldest son of George Lyell of Kinneff, died in Demerara on 3 December 1836. **[AJ#4640]**

LYON, ANTONIA EMILY WILLIAMS, born 1830, youngest daughter of Antony Menton Lyon, wife of William Hunter Campbell LL.D., died at Kitty House, East Coast, Demerara, 18 May 1871. [S#8700]

MACALASTER, JOHN, second son of John MacAlaster, Castlehead House, Paisley, Renfrewshire, married Katherine Lascelles Smith, second daughter of Reverend Francis Smith, in Buenos Ayres on 14 November 1877. [S#10,741]

MACALASTER, ..., daughter of John M. MacAlaster of the Mercantile Bank of the River Plate in Monte Video, was born on 15 September 1879. [S#11,312]

MACALLISTER, RANALD, third son of Dr MacAllister in Strathaird, Skye, died in Demerara on 31 March 1820. [BM#7.583]

MCANDIE, JAMES, in British Guiana, 1855. [NAS.242/70/6/183.Tain]

MCARA, ARCHIBALD, born 1804, son of James McAra (1768-1810) and Isabella Douglas (1778-1852), died in Valparaiso on 19 June 1846. [Cramond g/s, Midlothian]

MCARTHUR, DONALD, son of John McArthur of Ardgavannan, Argyll, an employee of Turnbull, Forbes and Company, died on his way home from Demerara on the schooner Diana, Captain Grieve, in July 1800. [NAS.CC2/8/105]; edict of executry, 1801. [NAS.CC2.8.105, 1]

MACARTHUR, ..., daughter of Charles MacArthur, was born in Georgetown, Demerara, on 21 September 1863. [S#2599]

MACARTHUR, ..., son of Charles MacArthur, was born in Georgetown, Demerara, on 9 April 1869. [S#8098]

MACARTNEY, ALEXANDER, second son of Reverend William MacArtney in Old Kirkpatrick, died in Arequibo on 3 December 1833. [SG#3/241]

MACARTNEY, JAMES, a merchant in Mexico, died in Edinburgh 22 August 1839, cnf 1839 Edinburgh [NAS.SC70.1.58/426]

MACARTNEY, WILLIAM, son of Reverend William MacCartney in Old Kilpatrick, Dunbartonshire, died in Gualaguaychiu Entre Rios on 30 August 1862. [S#2462]

MCAULAY, JAMES, late in Honduras, died in Exeter during 1795. [GM.65.174]

MACBEAN, AENEAS, son of William MacBean in Kirkcudbright, was drowned, along with his wife and only son, at Samanca, Peru, on 30 January 1881. [S#11,767]

MACBEAN, SAMUEL, son of William MacBean in Kirkcudbright, died in Lima on 15 April 1872. [S#8975]

MCBEAN, WILLIAM MCCAUL, second son of William McBean in Kirkcudbright, died in Rosario Sante Fe on 4 December 1867. [S#7657]

MACBEAN, ..., daughter of Aeneas MacBean, was born in Lima 16 August 1871. [S#8795]

MCBEATH, Dr WILLIAM, born in Inverness on 25 February 1764, a physician in Demerara, died on 11 October 1797. [Chapel Yard g/s, Inverness]

MCCALMONT, HUGH, born 1801, died 1838 in Demerara. [St Andrew's Scots Church g/s, Demerara]

MCCLELLAN, Reverend ALEXANDER, son of George McClellan [1783-1835] and Elizabeth Gordon in Borgue, Kirkcudbright, minister of St James, Demerara, 1862, died on 17 May 1868. [TMG#1/280; 2/372]

MCCLELLAND, JOHN, died in San Salvador during August 1832, cnf Edinburgh 1835.

MCCLURE, WILLIAM, born in Ayr 17 October 1763, son of David McClure and his wife Ann Kennedy, a geologist, died in San Angel, Mexico, 23 March 1840. [WA]

MCCLYMONT, JAMES, born 1786, son of James McClymont [1754-1829] and Agnes Logan [1766-1834], died in Colonia on the River Plate 30 June 1815. [Maybole Kirk Wynd g/s, Ayrshire]

MCCLYMONT, JOHN, born 1800, a farmer, with his wife Catherine and two children, emigrated from Leith to Argentina on the

Symmetry, master William Cochrane, on 22 May 1825.
[SSP#18]

MCCORQUDALE, ALEXANDER, in South America before 1844.
[NAS.GD18.364]

MCCREA, HENRY MITCHELL, died in Agua Santa, Pisagua, Peru,
14 July 1885. [Barrhill g/s, Ayrshire]

MCCREDIE, JOHN, born 1857, son of Alexander McCredie and
Ann McClelland, died in Montevideo 18 April 1888. [Girvan
g/s, Ayrshire]

MCCULLOCH, JOHN, in sugar estate Unidad, Partido de
Calabazar, Sagua la Grande, Cuba, cnf Edinburgh 1888.
[NAS.SC70.1.264/338]

MCCULLOCH, WILLIAM, a merchant in Vera Cruz, died at sea in
August 1848. Cnf Edinburgh 1850

MCCUNE, THOMAS, son of Samuel McCune in Wigtownshire,
educated at Glasgow University, a minister in British Guiana
in 1845. [F.7.675]

MCDONALD, A., in Demerara, around 1830. [NAS.GD1.641.49]

MCDONALD, ALEXANDER, educated at Aberdeen University,
minister of St Mary's, British Guiana 1838-1841. [F.7.679]

MCDONALD, ALEXANDER, a minister in Buenos Ayres in 1889.
[F#7.682]

MCDONALD, ALLAN, late in Berbice, Demerara, died 3 May 1849.
[Duddingston g/s]

MACDONALD, CHARLES, emigrated from Cromarty on the Planet
of London, Captain William Barclay, on 1 October 1825,
landed at La Guayra on 2 December 1825, settled at Topo,
Columbia, by 1827. [PRO.FO.18/47; FO.199/3/32]

MACDONALD, CHARLES, a farmer in Argentina, cnf 1881
Edinburgh. [NAS.SC70.1.207/874]

MCDONALD, DONALD, a student in Holland, then a Revenue
Officer in Demerara and in Berbice, 1817-1834.
[NAS.GD1.4.96]

MCDONALD, DONALD, brother of Clanranald, died in Berbice in
February 1838. [AJ#4717]

MCDONALD, GORDON, of Plantation Moy, Corome, Surinam, died
in Burntisland, Fife, on 28 June 1859. [Burntisland g/s]

MCDONALD, JOHN, in Berbice, son of the late Donald McDonald sometime in Jamaica, 1809. [NAS.RD2.307.259]

MCDONALD, NORMAN, born 1855, son of William Hamilton McDonald, Greenknowe, Bothwell, Lanarkshire, died in Buenos Ayres on 15 June 1879. [S#11,237]

MCDONALD, WILLIAM, in Demerara, around 1830. [NAS.GD1.641.49]

MCDONALD, Mrs ...., widow of John McDonald of Plantation Kintyre, Berbice, married Alexander McDuff, a Lieutenant of the 100th Regiment of Foot, on 18 November 1824. [S#508.829]

MACDONNELL, ALEXANDER, with his wife, and children George born 1797, Rebecca born 1805, Margaret born 1807, and Mary born 1809, emigrated from Cromarty on the <u>Planet of London</u>, Captain William Barclay, on 1 October 1825, landed at La Guayra on 2 December 1825, settled at Topo, Columbia, by 1827, finally settled in Guelph, Canada. [PRO.FO.18/47; FO.199/3/32]

MCDONNELL, HUGH, with his wife, and children Alexander born 1808, Janet born 1810, Margaret born 1812, Allen born 1815, and Mary born 1820, emigrated from Cromarty on the <u>Planet of London</u>, Captain William Barclay, on 1 October 1825, landed at La Guayra on 2 December 1825, settled Topo, Columbia, moved to Guelph, Canada, in 1827. [PRO.FO.18/47; FO.199/3/32]

MCDONELL, JOSEPH, with his wife, and children Elizabeth born 1812, Janet born 1814, Walter born 1816, Alexander born 1818, Catherine born 1820, and John born 1822, emigrated from Cromarty on the <u>Planet of London</u>, Captain William Barclay, on 1 October 1825, landed at La Guayra on 2 December 1825, settled at Topo, Columbia, by 1827. [PRO.FO.18/47; FO.199/3/32]

MCDOUGALL, DONALD, in Buenos Ayres, died 15 August 1859. Cnf Edinburgh 1860

MCDOUGALL, JAMES, born 1846, a joiner, third son of James McDougall in Eskdalerig, St Mungo, died in Georgetown, Demerara, on 8 October 1881. [AO:18.11.1881]

MCDOUGALL, JOHN, from Buenos Ayres, married Susan, daughter of Ronald Campbell of Auchenbreck, in Drimsynie on 4 July 1827. [DPCA#1356]

MCEWAN, ALEXANDER LOW, in Essequibo, British Guiana, grandson of Alexander Low, a merchant in Aberdeen, who died 26 February 1863. [NAS.SH.26.9.1885]

MCEWAN, JOHN, born 1806, son of William McEwan (1768-1832), died in Mexico 1832. [Logerait g/s, Perthshire]

MACFADYEN, JAMES, of the National Bank of Chile, married Isabella Wallace Honeyman, only daughter of Thomas Honeyman, Veitch Park, Haddington, East Lothian, at 233 Calle de Victoria, Valparaiso, in 1869. [S#8087]

MCFADZEAN, ..., daughter of James McFadzean of the National Bank of Chile, was born at 3 Rerynolds Buildings, Valparaiso, 19 April 1870. [S#8387]

MCFADYEAN, EMMA MARY, daughter of James McFadyean, was born in Valparaiso on 13 February 1874, died 12 October 1877. [S#9577/10,724]

MCFADYEAN, ..., son of James McFadyean of the National Bank of Chile, was born in Valparaiso on 12 December 1876. [S#10,462]

MACFARLANE, Reverend ANDREW, assistant to Reverend Dr Struthers, died in Georgetown, Demerara, on 5 September 1839. [AJ#4974][SG#8/815]

MCFARLANE, HELEN, eldest daughter of P.McFarlane, Faslane, Dunbartonshire, married Robert Smith MD, in Berbice on 28 June 1839. [SG#8/809]

MCFARLANE, JAMES, in Demerara, 1845. [NAS.RD5.758.681]

MACFARLANE, PETER, late rector of Leith High School, died in Monte Video 8 September 1870. [S#8512]; cnf 1871 Edinburgh. [NAS.SC70.1.151/94]

MACFARLANE, ..., daughter of Dr MacFarlane, was born in Gongo Soco on 11 January 1829. [S#967.239]

MCFARLIN, NORMAN MCLEOD, a merchant late of Manturin, South America, died 14 June 1853. Cnf Edinburgh 1854

MCFARQUHAR, GEORGE, eldest son of John McFarquhar a Writer to the Signet, died in Valparaiso, Chile, on 23 July 1823. [BM#15.131]

MCFARQUHAR, JOHN L., married Catherine Dampier, daughter of Reverend John Dampier, Dorset, in Rio de Janeiro on 1 March 1825. [BM#18.266]

MCFARQUHAR, JOHN, Bellevue, late of Demerara, died in Greenock on 26 September 1839. [SG#8/816]

MCGHONACHIE, JOHN, son of George McGhonachie, schoolmaster in Logie-Pert (died 1844) and Helen Rennie (died 1846, died in Honduras on 13 September 1832. [Pert g/s, Angus]

MACGILL, JOHN WHYTE, born in Musselburgh 21 August 1867, son of Henry Moncrieff Macgill. Educated at Edinburgh University MA, 1889, minister in British Guiana 1897-1924. [F.6.225]; married Edith Luxton Wreford, second daughter of S. Wreford, New Amsterdam, at All Saints Scots Church, New Amsterdam, British Guiana, in 1899. [S#17,364]

MCGILL, ..., daughter of Alexander McGill was born in Georgetown, Demerara, on 8 August 1874. [EC#28106]

MACGILL, ..., daughter of Archibald MacGill, was born in Georgetown, Demerara, on 8 October 1874. [S#9757]

MCGOUN, ARCHIBALD, born in 1809, son of Duncan MacGoun in Glasgow, Director of the Bote Mining Company, died in Zacatecas, Mexico, on 29 October 1878. [EC#29400] [S#11,016]; possibly from Renfrewshire, settled in Mexico by 1871. [NAS.SH.22.3.1871]

MCGOUN, JOHN STUART, MD, died in Acapulco, Mexico, during 1851. [NAS.SH.23.1.1871][S.17.1.1852]

MCGOUN, LAUCHLAN CAMPBELL, born 1817, son of Duncan McGoun a merchant in Glasgow, matriculated at Glasgow University 1831, in New York pre 1850, settled in Guanaxuhato, Mexico, by 1870; he married Ellen Bell in Edinburgh 30 January 1868 who died at Guanaxuata on 4 January 1869. [NAS.SH.14.12.1870; 22.3.1871] [MAGU#12869][ANY.2.229]

MCGOWAN, WILLIAM, Costa del Picador, near Porongos, Uruguay, 1887. [NAS.SC70.11.259/725]

MCGREGOR, CATHERINE CAMPBELL, eldest daughter of Alexander McGregor, St Andrew Square, Edinburgh, married

Ewen McPherson from Demerara, in Edinburgh during 1817. [S#17.17]

MCGREGOR, CATHERINE, youngest daughter of Rob Roy McGregor, Foss, Perthshire, married Duncan Campbell, Rosario de Santa Fe, late of Killin in perthshire, at 334 Calle St Martin, Buenos Ayres, in 1868. [S#7872]

MCGREGOR, D., from Kirkcaldy, Fife, emigrated to South America in June 1877. [FA, 2.6.1877]

MCGREGOR, DUNCAN, born 1811, died La Bonne Intention Estate, Demerara, July 1844. [Faslane g/s]

MACGREGOR, Sir GREGOR, born 1786, Cacique of Poyais on the Mosquito Shore, married Josepha Lobera, niece of Simon Bolivar, in Venezuela 1812. [NAS.GD50.184.84.30]; in Poyais 1830s. [NAS.GD50.184.104]

MCGREGOR, JAMES, a merchant, only son of Mr McGregor, St Andrew Square, Edinburgh, died in Georgetown, Demerara, on 10 June 1825. [BM#18.655]

MACGREGOR, JAMES SCOTT, born 1847, son of John McGregor of the Royal Hotel in Dundee, and nephew of Robert Scott of the Spread Eagle Hotel in Jedburgh, Roxburghshire, died in Demerara on 2 July 1874. [S#9678]

MCGREGOR, JOHN ANDERSON, born 1868, second son of James McGregor from Edinburgh, died in Santiago de Chili, 25 July 1870. [S#8478]

MCGREGOR, or WATT, MARY, in Argentina, 1890. [NAS.RS.Forfar.50.95]

MCGRIGOR, DAVID, born during 1799, son of Alexander McGrigor and Ann Mackay, a house carpenter at La Belle Alliance, Demerara, died 15 September 1839. [Croick g/s]

MCGROUTHER, Mrs SOPHIA SUSAN, born 1828, widow of James McGrouther late of Rio de Janeiro, died in Pau, Basses Pyrenees, on 4 April 1881. [S#11,773]

MCGUFFIE, JAMES MUIR, HM Consul in Gonaives, Haiti, died in New York 30 August 1849. [GM.ns32/559]

MCGUFFIE, JOHN, minister of St Saviour's, British Guiana, 1862-1878. [F.7.680]

MCHARDY, ..., emigrated from Cromarty on the Planet of London, Captain William Barclay, on 1 October 1825, landed at La

Guayra on 2 December 1825, settled at Topo, Columbia, by 1827. [PRO.FO.18/47; FO.199/3/32]

MCHARDY, ..., emigrated from Cromarty on the Planet of London, Captain William Barclay, on 1 October 1825, landed at La Guayra on 2 December 1825, settled at Topo, Columbia, by 1827. [PRO.FO.18/47; FO.199/3/32]

MACKINLAY, A. U., Director of the Commercial Bank of the River Plate, and of Bates, Stokes and Company of Buenos Ayres and Monte Video, 1872. [S#9025]

MCINROY, DAVID, third son of James Patrick McInroy of Lude and Margaret Seton Lillie, born 29 July 1831, died in San Jorge, Banda Oriental, on 23 March 1868. [Kilmaveonaig g/s, Blair Atholl, Perthshire]

MCINROY, JAMES, from Demerara, married Elizabeth Moore from St Eustatia, in Broomloan on 25 December 1797. [EEC#420]

MCINROY, ..., a planter at Phoenix Park, Demerara, before 1833. [NAS.GD132/796]

MACKINTOSH, CATHERINE, daughter of Alexander Mackintosh in Paramaribo, Surinam, married Johan Leng Hutchler, in Nymegen, the Netherlands, on 1 November 1876. [S#10,390]

MACINTOSH, CHARLES, born 1782, eldest son of Alexander MacIntosh and Janet McLean, drowned in the River Essequibo on 21 April 1814. [Inverness, Greyfriars, g/s]

MCINTOSH, DONALD, educated at King's College, Aberdeen, minister of St Mark's, British Guiana, 1829-1837. [F.7.679]

MCINTOSH, HENRY, 1675, a planter from Surinam, married Elizabeth Le Hunt from Port Royal, Jamaica, in 1688, settled in Surinam, died there in 1690. [CSP.1675.01][Abstracts of NY Wills, Liber 1-2, pp184-186][SPAWI.1675/401; 1676/943]

MACKINTOSH, LOUIS ALEXANDER, H.M.Consul, married Isabella Bathgate Marr, third daughter of James Marr of Alderston MD, MRCPE. in Paramaribo, Dutch Guina, on 4 January 1871. [S#8580]

MACINTOSH, PHINEAS, born 1784, second son of Alexander MacIntosh and Janet McLean, died in Demerara on 4 December 1805. [Inverness, Greyfriars, g/s]

MACKINTOSH, THOMAS, in Guadaloupe y Calvo, Mexico, 1853. [GM.NS.40.522]

MACKINTOSH,......, son of Louis Alexander Mackintosh, was born in Surinam on 1 June 1872. [S#9025]

MCINTYRE, J., minister in Bahia Blanca, Argentina, 1897. [F.7.682]

MCINTYRE, J. J., from Glasgow, in Buenos Ayres 1818-1821. [NLS.Acc.4701]

MCINTYRE, ..., daughter of Dr John McIntyre was born in Tranquillity House, Moro Velho, Brazil, on 29 January 1868. [S#7678]

MACKAY, AENEAS, son of James Mackay in Ross-shire, died in Havanna, Cuba, in May 1817. [GM#61/186]

MACKAY, ALEXANDER, born 1796, late in Rio de Janeiro, died at Bromley, Montrose, Angus, 3 March 1843. [AJ#4966]

MCKAY, ALEXANDER, from Leith, then in Altoda, Tahuel, Chile, married Jeannie Brunton, eldest daughter of George Brunton in Valparaiso, there on 11 December 1872. [S#8918]

MACKAY, DANIEL, from Santa Cruz, married Mrs John Muir, a widow in Demerara, in Edinburgh on 17 February 1825. [GM#95/273]

MACKAY, DONALD, in Demerara, 1802. [NAS.GD23.6.391]

MCKAY, ROBERT, vice consul at Maracaibo, 1846. [NAS.242/70/5/229.Tain]

MCKECHNIE, JOHN, a medical student in Edinburgh, then a physician in Demerara 1809. [NAS.CS17.1.20/511]

MCKENZIE, ALEXANDER, LL.D., born 1770, died 1828 in Demerara. [St Andrew's Scots Church g/s, Demerara]

MCKENZIE, CHARLES GORDON, a minister in Buenos Ayres from 1899 to 1902. [F#7.682]

MCKENZIE, Miss JANE, late in Demerara, died in Edinburgh 3 September 1825, cnf Edinburgh 1836.

MCKENZIE, JOHN, third son of Charles McKenzie a writer in Edinburgh, died in Demerara during 1802. [GkAd#54]

MCKIDDIE, W., born 1842, died in Buenos Ayres in 1871. [SRP#365]

MCKINLAY, HELEN, eldest daughter of William McKinley in Buenos Ayres, married Henry Graham Wilding, youngest son of Harry Wilding of Liverpool, in Buenos Ayres on 10 April 1878. [EC#29213]

MCKINNELL, ROBERT, in Buenos Ayres, 1898. [NAS.RS.Whithorn #8.3]

MACKINTOSH, EWAN CLARK, born 1811, died in Tacubaya, Mexico, 7 May 1861. [S#1885]

MACKINTOSH, HENRY ALEXANDER, born during 1808, died in Mineral de la Luz, Mexico, on 3 September 1860. [DC#23550]

MCINTOSH, JOHN, born 1864, from Braenalion, Glencairn, Ballater, Aberdeenshire, died in San Jose de Guatamala, Mexico, on 6 March 1900. [AJ:17.4.1900]; sometime of Hakalan, Hawaii, died in San Jose de Guatamala, Mexico, cnf Edinburgh 1900. [NAS.SC70.1.392/295]

MACKINTOSH, MARION SUSAN ANNE READE, only daughter of Thomas Mackintosh in Guadaloupe y Calvo, Mexico, married William Randolph Simpson, RA, in Southsea, 13 August 1853. [GM.ns40/522]

MACKINTOSH, RONALD MARR, an infant and second son of Louis A. Mackintosh, died in Paramaribo, Dutch Guiana, on 8 October 1874. [S#9776]

MCINTOSH, WILLIAM, son of Alexander McIntosh [1769-1802] a merchant in Inverness, settled in Surinam before 1843.[Kilmallie g/s]

MACKINTOSH, WILLIAM LYSTER HAY, born 1824, died in Guanasevi, Mexico, 21 May 1856. [GM#ns2/1.390]

MCINTYRE, JOHN, formerly a merchant in Liverpool, died in Demerara on 4 July 1824. [S#487.666]

MCINTYRE, PATRICK, died in Demerara on 12 August 1821. [BM#10.489]

MCISAAC, WILLIAM, a merchant in Valparaiso, cnf 1879 Edinburgh. [NAS.SC70.1.197/1054]

MACKAY, ALEXANDER, born in 1841, son of George Mackay, died in Panama on 14 August 1888. [Chapel Yard /s, Inverness]

MACKAY, MARIANNE CAMERON, fourth daughter of Robert Mackay in Fort William, married Thomas Powditch of Caldera, in Valparaiso, Chile, on 29 April 1854. [EEC#22604]

MCKENZIE, ALEXANDER, born around 1783, second son of George McKenzie of Pitlundy, died in Demerara during 1802. [SM#44.448]

MCKENZIE, Dr ALEXANDER, died in Demerara on 15 September 1828. [BM#25.268]

MCKENZIE, CHARLES, died in Demerara on 13 May 1839. [SG#8/783]

MACKENZIE, DEVONIA, wife of George Knox, died in Georgetown, Demerara, on 25 January 1868. [S#7672]

MCKENZIE, HUGH, born 1821, son of Reverend David McKenzie, died in Demerara during 1844. [Farr g/s]

MCKENZIE, HUGH, an engineer, born during 1835 in Kinghorn, Fife, died in Eten, Peru, on 7 November 1875. [PJ]

MCKENZIE, JANE, late in Demerara, then in Edinburgh, died on 3 September 1835. Cnf Edinburgh 1836

MCKENZIE, JOHN, a joiner, emigrated from Cromarty on the Planet of London, Captain William Barclay, on 1 October 1825, landed at La Guayra on 2 December 1825, settled at Topo, Columbia, by 1827, later moved to Caracas. [PRO.FO.18/47; FO.199/3/32]

MCKENZIE, Dr SIMON, in Jamaica, son of Dr John McKenzie, Fortrose, Ross-shire, died in Fortrose, Honduras, on 2 August 1797. [SM#49.621]

MCKENZIE, WILLIAM, born 1847, son of William McKenzie and Jane Thompson in Carron, died in Surinam on 10 December 1893. [Aberlour g/s, Banffshire]

MACKIE, Reverend JAMES, born in 1820, son of George Mackie in Hillhead of Blackchambers, Kinellar, Aberdeenshire, former minister of Buckie, died at St Mark's, Demerara, on 14 April 1876. [AJ#6702][F.7.678]

MACKINLAY, A.U., Director of the Commercial Bank of the River Plate, and of Bates, Stokes and Company in Buenos Ayres and in Monte Video, 1872. [S#9025]

MACKINLAY, JAMES B., a broker and commission agent in Buenos Ayres, married Christian, second daughter of John McLeod, Tyningham, East Lothian, in Salta, Argentina, 3 September 1872. [S#9149]

MCKINLEY, MARGARET GLEN, wife of Reverend John Currie, died in Smith Church Manse, Georgetown, Demerara, on 30 July 1881. [S#11,894]

MCKINNON, DAVID REID, born 1861, MB, CM, FRCS, eldest son of Surgeon General David McKinnon, Keith Lodge, Stonehaven,Kincardineshire, died in Belize during 1890. [AJ:17.10.1890]

MCKINNON, JOHN, a merchant at the Bay of Honduras, co-partner of Roger Gale, 1768, 1775. [NAS.AC8.1828; AC7.55]

MACKINNON, JOHN, born 1824, died 1852 in Demerara. [St Andrew's Scots Church g/s, Demerara]

MACKRAY, PATRICK, a merchant in Demerara, eldest son of Robert Mackray a manufacturer in Aberdeen, 1824. [NAS.RD5.275.8]; born in Aberdeen, died in Georgetown, Demerara, 1835. [AJ:22.7.1835]

MCLACHLAN, ANGUS, master of the brig Heyworth of Greenock, died in Georgetown, Demerara, on 3 November 1841. [GH#4062]

MACLAGAN, Dr DAVID PHILIP, assistant surgeon on HMS Icarus, eldest son of Dr Douglas MacLagan PRCS Edinburgh, died in Ruatan Bay Islands, Honduras, 27 June 1860. [S#1591] [DC#23522]

MCLAGGAN, HENRY, born 1776, a carpenter, late in Demerara, died in Stix, Perthshire, 14 February 1827. [Kenmore g/s, Perthshire]

MCLAREN, PETER M. WATSON, in British Guina, cnf 1878 Edinburgh. [NAS.SC70.1.189/151]

MCLAREN, ROBERT, a merchant in Demerara, died on his passage home on 6 June 1820. [BM#7.584]

MCLAREN, THOMAS, planter in Demerara 1814. [NAS.RD4.237.901]

MCLAUCHLAN, DUNCAN, sometime of Perth, Dundee, Monifieth and Edinburgh, engineer and superintendent of the Callao Gasworks, died in Callao, Peru, on 4 May 1868. [S#7763]

MCLEA, DANIEL, born 1803, son of Kenneth McLea, skipper in Greenock, and Jean McVicar, died in Buenos Ayres 21 January 1833. [Inverkip, Greenock, g/s]

MCLEAN, JOHN, son of John McLean a merchant in Glasgow, educated at Glasgow University around 1794, died at the Bay of Honduras on 14 March 1806. [MAGU#176][SM#68.486]

MCLEAN, JOHN, eldest son of John McLean a merchant in Glasgow, educated at Glasgow University in 1794, died at the Bay of Honduras on 14 March 1806. [MAGU#176]

MCLEAN, JOHN, a merchant, married Senora Rosa Echanes from Lima, there on 2 June 1824. [S#521.16]

MCLEAN, JOHN ALLAN, from Glasgow and London, a railway manager in Cuba, cnf Edinburgh 1900. [NAS.SC70.1.396/268]

MCLEAN, MARGARET born 1827, died in Buenos Ayres in 1871. [SRP#365]

MCLEAN, PATRICK, born in Gorbals, Glasgow, on 25 April 1807, son of Reverend James McLean and Ann Ballantyne, a merchant in Buenos Ayres, died 3 February 1855. [F.3.409]

MCLEAN, ROBERT CRAWFORD, born in Gorbals, Glasgow, on 21 November 1811, son of Reverend James McLean and Ann Ballantyne, a merchant in Monte Video and in Manchester, died on 29 April 1870. [F.3.409]

MCLEAN, Mrs S. born 1797, from Inverness, died in Buenos Ayres in 1871. [SRP#365]

MACLEAN,........, son of Peter MacLean late of Rankeillor Hope, Fife, was born in Fitzroy, Port Stanley, Falkland Islands, on 22 March 1889. [FFP]

MACLELLAN, Rev. ALEXANDER, minister of St James, British Guiana, 1862, died there 17 May 1868. [S#7762][F.7.677]

MCLELLAN, SAMUEL HANNAY, born 1839, third son of W. H. McLellan of Marks, Kirkcudbright, died on the Estancia Alto Redondo, Monte, Buenos Ayres, on 30 january 1868. [S#7698]

MCLENNAN, ALEXANDER STEWART, second son of R. McLennan in Pollewe, Ross-shire, died in Demerara on 5 May 1838. [AJ#4724][SG#7/683]

MACLENNAN, GARDNER WYLDE, born 1866, son of Alexander MacLennan, 1 Buckingham Street, Glasgow, died at Estancia Fortin Lavalle, Rocha, Buenos Ayres, on 10 December 1898. [S#17334]

MCLEOD, HUGH, in Georgetown, Demerara, died on 7 February 1839, cnf Edinburgh 1841

MCLEOD, JOHN, with his wife, and daughter Mary born 1818, emigrated from Cromarty on the Planet of London, Captain

William Barclay, on 1 October 1825, landed at La Guayra on 2 December 1825, settled at Topo, Columbia, by 1827. [PRO.FO.18/47; FO.199/3/32]

MCLEOD, CHRISTIAN, second daughter of John McLeod, Tyningham, East Lothian, married James B. Mackinlay, a broker and commission agent in Buenos Ayres, in Salta, Argentina, 3 September 1872. [S#9149]

MCLEROTH, ROBERT, born June 1792, son of Captain Thomas McLeroth, Lieutenant of the 63rd Regiment, died in Surinam 20 October 1809. [South Queensferry g/s]

MCLETCHIE, CATHERINA DALZELL, third daughter of Robert McLetchie in Old Cumnock, Ayrshire, married William Martin Middleton, a merchant in Berbice, at Windsor Villa, Georgetown, Demerara, 10 February 1871. [S#8622]

MCMILLAN, JOHN, second son of John McMillan of Edinburgh High School, married Elizabeth Barry Craswell, eldest daughter of William Craswell, in Monte Video on 15 July 1863. [S#2561]

MCMINN, ALEXANDER, a merchant, youngest son of John McMinn in Crofts of Crossmichael, died in Buenos Ayres on 4 June 1812. [SM#74.805]

MCNAIR, ..., son of Archibald McNair, was born in Bahia, Brazil, on 23 June 1879. [EC#29583]

MCNEILE, JOHN, a merchant, married Donna Pasquella de las Talegas, in Buenos Ayres on 1 July 1813. [EA#5196.13]

MCNEILL, CHARLES, from Demerara, son of Captain Alexander McNeill of Colonsay, married Margaret, only child of Malcolm McNeill of Lossit, in Glasgow on 5 November 1840. [W#88]

MCNEILL, JOHN HENRY HORTON, a minister in Buenos Ayres from 1897-1899. [F#7.682]

MCNEILL, LACHLAN, born on 22 April 1834, third son of Lachlan McNeill, farmer in Kilmun, and Jane Black, educated at Glasgow University and at St Andrews University, a missionary in Banda Oriental, Uruguay, from 1866 to 1877, a minister in Buenos Ayres, Argentina, from 1883, died in England on 18 December 1917. [F.7.683]

MCNIE, ROBERT LAMOND, minister of St Mary's, British Guiana, 1897-. [F.7.679]

MCNIVEN, DANIEL, in Almacende Fee, Santiago, Chile, 1875. [NAS.SC49.48.25.75/47]

MCNIVEN, WILLIAM RUTHERFORD, eldest son of Allan McNiven, married Umbelina Da Ameral, youngest daughter of Mr Alvim, a coffee planter, in Rio de Janeiro on 6 November 1871. [S#8876]

MCNIVEN, Mrs UMBELINA AMERAL, daughter of Miguel de Souza Mello e Alvim of the Imperial Brazilian Navy, wife of Rutherford McNiven, died in Rio de Janeiro 10 August 1872. [S#9093]

MCPHEE, ALEXANDER, with his wife, and children Donald born 1807, John born 1809, Duncan born 1811, Sarah born 1816, and Alexander born 1821, emigrated from Cromarty on the <u>Planet of London</u>, Captain William Barclay, on 1 October 1825, landed at La Guayra on 2 December 1825, settled at Topo, Columbia, by 1827. [PRO.FO.18/47; FO.199/3/32]

MCPHERSON, EWEN, from Demerara, married Catherine Campbell McGregor, eldest daughter of Alexander McGregor, St Andrew Square, Edinburgh, in Edinburgh during 1817. [S#17.17]

MCPHERSON, JAMES, born 1783, late in Essequibo, died in Perth 13 March 1848. [Perth, Greyfriars, g/s]

MCPHERSON, MUNGO, in Hampton Court Plantation, British Guiana, died in Demerara on 10 August 1848. Cnf Edinburgh 1850

MCPHERSON, SOPHIA CRIBBES, youngest daughter of Alexander McPherson, died in Valparaiso, Chile, on 13 October 1877. [S#10,729]

MCPHERSON, WILLIAM, son of Allan McPherson and Elizabeth McPherson in Blairgowrie, Perthshire, a planter in Berbice around 1806. [NAS.NRAS.bundle 8/10]

MCPHION, PETER, second son of Peter McPhion a merchant in Glasgow, minister of St James, British Guiana, 1830-1852, died in England 1852. [F.7.677]

MACQUEEN, ..., daughter of William L. MacQueen, was born in Valparaiso, Chile, on 24 February 1877. [S#10,541]

MACQUEEN, ..., daughter of Archibald M. MacQueen, was born in Valparaiso, Chile, on 10 March 1877. [S#10,541]

MCQUEEN, WILLIAM LENNIE, born 1833, died in Valparaiso, Chile, on 23 January 1879. [Drymen g/s][S#11,092]

MACRAE, ALEXANDER, a Member of the Court of Policy of Demerara, and the Chief of his name in the Highlands, died in Demerara on 9 June 1812. [SM#74.727]

MCRAE, ALEXANDER, with his wife, and children Christiana born 1814, Rudolph born 1817, William born 1817, Alexander born 1818, and Duncan born 1820, emigrated from Cromarty on the Planet of London, Captain William Barclay, on 1 October 1825, landed at La Guayra on 2 December 1825, settled at Topo, Columbia, by 1827. [PRO.FO.18/47; FO.199/3/32]

MACRAE, ALEXANDER ARCHIBALD, son of Alexander MacRae, Demerara, died in Portobello on 10 July 1854. [EEC#22605]

MACRAE, ALEXANDER, late of Demerara, died in Southampton on 31 July 1860. [EEC#23525]

MACREDIE, Mrs ALICE ANNE, wife of William M. MacRedie, died in Nickerie, Surinam, on 19 August 1884. [S#12849]

MACREDIE,........., daughter of W. M. MacRedie, was born in Nickerie, Surinam, on 9 October 1881. [S#11,961]

MCSWINNEY, Mrs MARY ANNA, wife of John McSwinney a Stipendiary Magistrate, died in New Amsterdam, Berbice, on 3 October 1860. [DC#23553]

MCTAVISH, ALEXANDER, with his wife, and children Nancy born 1814, Mary born 1815, Catherine born 1818, Margaret born 1822, and Alexander born 1825, emigrated from Cromarty on the Planet of London, Captain William Barclay, on 1 October 1825, landed at La Guayra on 2 December 1825, settled at Topo, Columbia, by 1827. [PRO.FO.18/47; FO.199/3/32]

MCTAVISH, DUNCAN, born 1864, son of John McTavish and Helen McGillvray, died in October 1904, buried in Gallag, Peru. [Golspie g/s]

MCTAVISH, HUGH, a sheep farmer in Buenos Ayres, cnf 1873 Edinburgh. [NAS.SC70.1.165/579]

MACVICAR, C. R. DAVIDSON, of Cyrilton and Dearg, died in Vera Cruz on 2 October 1883. [S#12,556]

MACVICAR, DAVID ROBERTSON, from Edinburgh, sub-manager of the River Plate Trust Agency in Buenos Ayres, cnf Edinburgh 1900. [NAS.SC70.1.393/641]

MAILER, ROBERT, son of John Mailer [1796-1857] a builder in Alloa, and Elizabeth Blair [1802-1870], settled in Rosano de Santa fe, Mexico, by 1872. [Alloa g/s]

MAIR, JAMES HUNTER, MD, born 1798, son of Dr James H. Mair and Marion ..., died in Buenos Ayres on 21 December 1826. [BM#21.773][Ayr g/s]

MAIR, Dr WILLIAM, from Edinburgh, died in Buenos Ayres on 10 July 1869. [S#8141]

MAITLAND, DAVID, minister of St Marks, British Guiana, 1866, died 18 February 1875. [F.7.678]

MALCOLM, JOHN, born 1856, from Falkirk, Stirlingshire, manager of Vryheid's Lust Estate, Demerara, died in 1881. [S#11,968]

MANSON, EMMA, in Georgetown, Demerara, 1842. [NAS.RS.Tain.5.34]

MANSON, JOHN, husband of Jessie Smith, 25 Gray Street, Aberdeen, died in San Albino Gold Mines, Ocatalo Republic, Nicaragua, on 23 July 1900. [AJ:30.7.1900]

MARKS, CHARLES, an old man, emigrated from Cromarty on the Planet of London, Captain William Barclay, on 1 October 1825, landed at La Guayra on 2 December 1825, settled at Topo, Columbia, by 1827. [PRO.FO.18/47; FO.199/3/32]

MARSH, Mrs ...., wife of Thomas Marsh, died in Demerara on 27 July 1824. [BM#16.488]

MARSHALL, ALEXANDER, MD, in Demerara 1822. [NAS.CS17.1.42/41]

MARSHALL, JAMES, born in 1847, from Parkhead, Glasgow, died in the English Hospital, Buenos Ayres, on 29 July 1875. [EC#28367]

MARSHALL, JOHN BALLANTYNE, married Harriet Howard, in Santiago, Chile, on 25 August 1868. [S#7875]

MARSHALL, JOHN, from Kirkcaldy, married Jemima Smith Mackay, youngest daughter of William Mackay a cork manufacturer in Edinburgh, at Estancia Sajones, Buenos Ayres, on 19 November 1872. [FH][S#9194]

MARSHALL, PETER, from Govan, son of David Marshall a spirit merchant in Edinburgh, was drowned in the wreck of the steamer Atacama off the coast of Chile in 1877. [S#10.761]

MARSHALL, ..., son of John Marshall, was born at Estancia Via Monte, Buenos Ayres, on 22 August 1873. [S#9438]

MARTIN, NICOL, MD, in Demerara, 1844. [NAS.RS38.GR2249/16]

MARTIN, SIMON GERARD, in Demerara, then in Glasgow, cnf 27 October 1814 Glasgow. [NAS.CC9.7.78.594]

MARTIN, THOMAS, a merchant, died in Demerara on 10 December 1820. [BM#8.708]

MARTIN, WILLIAM, an engineer in Valparaiso, Chile, 1884. [NAS.SC58.59.29.235]

MASON, ELMA MERCEDES, daughter of John Mason, died in Callao on 28 December 1867. [S#7668]

MASON, JOHN, from Leith, died in Santos, Brazil, on 1 September 1863. [S#2592]

MASSON, JAMES, born 1849, son of Alexander Masson in Harthills, Kintore, Aberdeenshire, died in Berbice, British Guina, on 24 January 1875. [AJ:2.2.1875]

MATHER, GEORGE, in Buenos Ayres, 25 April 1857. [NAS.RS.Edinburgh.69/258]

MATHER, ROBERT ALEXANDER, a clerk in Bahia, Brazil, grandson of Alexander Mather a wright in Arbroath, Angus, who died on 22 January 1881. [NAS.SH]

MATHER, THOMAS, born during 1822, son of James Mather and Christine Melville, a shipmaster, died in the River Gallegos, South America, on 23 October 1850. [Ferryport-on-Craig g/s, Fife] [PR.22.3.1851]

MATHESON, ALEXANDER GORDON, youngest son of Colin Matheson of Bennetsfield, died in Berbice on 13 October 1820. [BM#8.482]

MATHESON, DUNCAN, son of John Matheson, settled in Demerara by 1844. [Struy, Inverness, g/s]

MATHESON, JOHN, son of John Matheson, settled in Demerara by 1844. [Struy, Inverness, g/s]

MATHESON, KENNETH, British vice-consul in Bolivar, Columbia, 1860. [NAS.GD219.347]

MATHESON, MARTHA FRASER, relict of Hugh Junor in Essequibo, 1850. [NAS.RS38.GR2481/189]

MATHESON, RODERICK, born 1814, son of John Matheson, 'many years in Demerara', died 20 February 1884. [Struy, Inverness, g/s]

MATHESON, WILLIAM J., of the Banco Anglo, Buenos Ayres, 1 October 1893. [NAS.RS.Lochmaben#12/200]

MATHESON, ..., son of Finlay Matheson, was born in Rio de Janeiro on 28 July 1878. [EC#29298]

MATHEW, JAMES, in Monte Video, 1883. [NAS.SC48.49.25.83/123]

MATHEW, THOMAS, formerly a spirit dealer in Glasgow, by February 1816 on Washington Estate, Berbice. [NAS.CS17.1.35/237]

MATHEW, ..., son of James Mathew, was born in Monte Video, Banda Oriental, on 28 February 1877. [S#10,517]

MATTHEWS, ALEXANDER, educated at St Andrews University, minister of St James, British Guiana, 1860, died in February 1862. [F.7.677]

MATHIESON, ..., son of Kenneth Mathieson, was born in Valparaiso, Chile, on 4 May 1877. [s#10,546]

MAULE, JOHN, a merchant in Demerara, son of Charles Maule in Leith, died in Demerara on 17 October 1798. [AJ#2664][GC#1159]

MAXTON, ANN ELIZA, eldest daughter of Robert Maxton in Saltcoats, Ayrshire, married Martin B. Cannon, in Buenos Ayres on 21 September 1868. [S#7878]

MAXTON, JANE MACGILL, daughter of Peter Maxton a shipowner in Greenock, married Robert Bryson, CE, in Lima on 21 February 1876. [S#10,203]

MAXWELL, P. B., born in 1844, a Magistrate and Sheriff of Berbice, eldest son of Sir P. B. Maxwell, died in New Amsterdam, British Guiana, on 18 October 1878. [EC#29374]

MELDRUM, ANDREW, in Georgetown, British Guina, 1856. [NAS.SC48.49.25.56/283]

MELDRUM, DAVID, born in Dundee on 22 February 1826, son of William Meldrum and Jane Millar, died in Rio de Janeiro on 15 May 1850. [Ferryport-on-Craig g/s, Fife]

MELROSE, THOMAS, born 1829, died Cocolapan, Orizaba, Mexico, on 26 April 1876. [S#10,254]

MELROSE, ..., son of D. A. Melrose, De Las Playas, was born in Buenos Ayres on 11 December 1868. [S#7957]

MELVILLE, ANDREW, a merchant in Mexico, 1844. [NAS.SH.8.5.1844]

MELVILLE, ANDREW, a merchant in Surinam, died pre 1844. [NAS.SH.8.5.1844]

MELVILLE, D., a merchant in Berbice, married Sarah, daughter of John Polson in Old Aberdeen, there on 31 January 1828. [S#846.114]

MELVILLE, Captain JAMES, from Anstruther, Fife, died in Rio de Janeiro on 15 September 1873. [S#9453]

MELVILLE, or KELLIE, Mrs MARY, from Elgin, Morayshire, then Estancia Maria Chascpmas, Buenos Ayres, cnf Edinburgh 1889. [NAS.SC70.1.274/594]

MELVILLE, ..., daughter of George Melville of the Colonial Civil Service, was born in Georgetown, Demerara, on 13 September 1877, survived a week. [S#10,683]

MELVILLE, ..., daughter of George Melville, was born at Bellfield Villa, Georgetown, Demerara, on 17 January 1879. [EC#29450]

MENTIPLAY, ANDREW, born 1850, from Addiewell, was drowned in the wreck of the Pacific Company's stemer Eten off Point Vantana, Chile, on 15 July 1877. [S#10,661]

MENZIES, Mrs JANE MARY, wife of Dr Menzies, died in Belgrano, Buenos Ayres, on 12 February 1878. [EC#299167]

MENZIES, ROBERT, born around 1799, son of William Menzies a wright in Glasgow, educated at Glasgow University, a minister in British Guiana 1837-1844, died 1844. [F.7.677]

MENZIES, ..., son of Reverend Robert Menzies of St Luires, was born on Plantation de Kinderon, Demerara, on 6 November 1841. [GH#4067]

MERRY, GEORGE, born in 1814, eldest son of George Merry a tobacconist in Edinburgh, died in Demerara on 27 February 1839. [SG#8/765]

MIDDLETON, WILLIAM MARTIN, a merchant in Berbice, married Catherina Dalzell McLetchie, third daughter of Robert McLetchie in Old Cumnock, Ayrshire, at Windsor Villa, Georgetown, Demerara, 10 February 1871. [S#8622]

MIDDLETON, ..., son of Harry Middleton was born in Sante Fe on the River Plate on 30 December 1873. [EC#27901]

MILLAR, ELIZABETH, third daughter of Andrew Millar, Writer to the Signet, married Richard James Andrew, from Belize, Honduras, in Edinburgh on 13 August 1828. [S#898.530]

MILLER, GEORGE XAVIER, born in 1835, son of Alexander and Jane Miller, died in Valparaiso on 24 January 1878. [EC#29166]

MILLER, JOHN, born 1787, a farmer, with his wife Anne and one child, emigrated from Leith to Argentina on the Symmetry, master William Cochrane, on 22 May 1825. [SRP#18]

MILLER, ..., daughter of James Miller was born in Georgetown, Demerara, on 22 April 1838. [SG#7/672]

MILLIE, CHARLES JAMES, son of David Reddie Millie, was born in Coquimbo, Chile, 25May 1872. [S#9039]; died there on 6 September 1872. [S#9132]

MILLIE, DAVID R., eldest son of William Millie in Pathhead, Kirkcaldy, Fife, married Rosalia Richardson, in Coquimbo, Chile, on 23 March 1869. [S#8074]

MILLIE, JAMES, youngest son of David R. Millie, died in Coquimba, Chile, on 16 February 1878. [S#10,838]

MILLIE, ..., daughter of T. J. W. Millie, was born in Coquimbo, Chile, on 23 November 1867. [S#7633]

MILLIE, ..., son of T. J. W. Millie, was born in Coquimbo, Chile, on 24 June 1869. [S#8126]

MILLIE, ..., son of David Reddie Millie, was born in Coquimbo, Chile, 10 April 1870. [S#8375]

MILLIE, ..., son of Thomas. J. W. Millie, was born in Coquinbo, Chile, on 11 February 1871. [S#8637]

MILLIE, ..., daughter of D. Reddie Millie, was born in Coquimbo, Chile, on 5 August 1873. [S#9418]

MILLIE, ..., son of D. R. Millie, was born in Coquimba, Chile, on 2 November 1876. [S#10,450]

MILLIGAN, ALEXANDER, in Rio de Janeiro, 23 July 1857. [NAS.RS.Annan#10/83]

MILLS, PETER DRUMMOND, son of John Milne or Mills a wheelwright in Perth, settled in Ponce, Porto Rico, by 1863. [NAS.SH.15.8.1863]

MILNE, ALEXANDER, born 1781, Lieutenant Colonel of the 19th Regiment, died in Demerara on 5 November 1827. [Demerara g/s]

MILNE, ALEXANDER, born in 1850 son of Alexander Milne and Mary Hastings, died in Lima on 11 August 1877. [Arbroath Abbey g/s, Angus]

MILNE, ELIZABETH, third daughter of James Milne late of Kirkland, married Captain Thomas Jones of the Brachvelo Works in Buenos Ayres on 3 March 1884. [PJ]

MILNE, HENRYb, born 1825, died in Buenos Ayres in 1871. [SRP#365]

MILNE, JOHN ALEXANDER RATCLIFFE, in San Pedro Sula, Honduras, cnf Edinburgh 1897. [NAS.SC70.1.355/376]

MILNE, MARTHA, daughter of James Milne late of Kirkland, wife of Robert Craig, died in Buenos Ayres on 8 February 1885. [PJ]

MILNE, PATRICK WILSON, son of Peter Milne (1815-1887), a baker in Edinburgh, and Isabella MacMillan (1818-1902), died in Para, Brazil, 14 July 1899. [East Preston Street cemetery, Edinburgh]

MITCHELL, DAVID, from Perth, died in Mahaica, Demerara, on 12 October 1839. [SG#833]

MITCHELL, JOHN GUNN, born 1877, died in Argentina on 27 October 1907. [Tongue g/s]

MOFFAT, ADAM P., born in 1841, from Mount Pleasant, Berwickshire, died in Cardoba on 11 April 1875. [EC#28292]

MOIR, JOHN, a mercantile clerk in Iquique, Peru, 1882. [NAS.SC58.42.51.975]

MOIR, WILLIAM, in Aberdeen, late in Brazil, 2 June 1821. [NAS.RGS#163/54]

MOIR, JOHN BARNET, son of J. Munro Moir, MD, was born in Belize, British Honduras, on 6 December 1881, died there on 25 January 1882. [S#12,003/12,050]

MOLLE, GEORGE CROWE, second son of William Molle of Mains, Writer to the Signet, died in Demerara on 21 February 1853. [EEC#22494]

MONRO, ALEXANDER, elder son of William Monro, Bloomfield Place, Glasgow, died in Demerara on 9 December 1881. [S#11,984]

MONTGOMERY, HENRY, born in 1852, only son of Archibald Montgomery in Belize, died on his plantation El Chagure, Costa Cuca, Guatamala, on 7 November 1874. [EC#28172]

MOONEY, JAMES, from Leith, died in Savannah, South America, cnf Edinburgh 1901. [NAS.SC70.1.402/265]

MOORE, Mrs MARY, born 1815, wife of John Moore, and mother of Mrs David Jack, 1 Morton Terrace, Mayfield, Edinburgh, died in Georgetown, Demerara, on 20 March 1882. [S#12,091]

MORN, DAVID, from Glasgow, married Marjory Stevenson, youngest daughter of Robert Stevenson a farmer in Auchanachie, Banffshire, in the British Consulate, Mexico City, 1859. [CM#21776]

MORRIS, ALEXANDER BRUCE, died in Berbice on 20 July 1808. [SM#70.796]

MORRISON, ALEXANDER, Lima, Peru, married Alice Dickson, daughter of Henry Dickson in Liverpool, in Lima on 27 August 1878. [S#10,982]

MORRISON, JANE, wife of James Robertson, died at Estancia Los Inglesias, Ajo, Buenos Ayres, on 22 April 1878. [S#10,884]

MORRISON, JOHN, in Real del Monte, Mexico, died 16 July 1853. Cnf Edinburgh 1856 [NAS.SH.4.6.1863; NAS.SC70.1.92/826]

MORRISON, JOHN J., from Leith, engineer of the Chilean Navy, married Isabella Denholm, daughter of James Denholm a merchant in Glasgow, in Valparaiso 19 July 1861. [S#1964]

MORRISON, WILLIAM, born 1792, son of Reverend Roderick Morrison and Jane Fraser in Kintail, died in Demerara on 15 May 1814. [Kiel Duich g/s, Wester Ross]

MORRISON, WILLIAM, born 1783, from Demerara, died in Aberdeen on 5 February 1859. [CM#21/647]

MORRISON, WILLIAM, infant son of Alexander Morrison, died in Lima, Peru, on 29 January 1883. [S#12,369]

MORRISON, ..., son of John S. Morrison an engineer from Leith, was born in Valparaiso, Chile, on 21 November 1875, died there on 28 August 1879. [S#10,133/11,314]

MORRISON, ..., son of John S. Morrison from Leith, was born in Valparaiso, Chile, on 11 June 1879. [S#11,254]

MORRISON, ..., son of Alexander Morrison, was born in Lima, Peru, on 4 July 1879. [S#11,255]

MORRISON,......, son of Alexander Morrison, was born 9 January 1881 on board the San Carlos off Callao, a temporary residence in consequence of the impending attack of Chilean forces on Lima. [S#11,731]

MORRISON,......, son of John S. Morrison from Leith, was born in Valparaiso on 10 February 1881. [S#11,761]

MOUAT, TADEA CHRISTINA, daughter of John Mouat in Valparaiso, married John Henry Toyne, in London 25 September 1861. [S#1958]

MOWAT, JAMES, third son of James Mowat a merchant in Aberdeen, died in Demerara on 21 January 1838. [AJ#4710]; cnf 1848 Edinburgh

MUIR, ANDREW WRIGHT, a bank clerk in Santos, Brazil, cnf Edinburgh 1892. [NAS.SC70.1.311/745]

MUIR, JAMES, of Todd, Muir and Company, died in Vera Cruz on 6 September 1834. [SG#2/192]

MUIR, JAMES, in Georgetown, British Guina, cnf 1878 Edinburgh. [NAS.SC70.1.190/36]

MUIR, JAMES, minister of St James, British Guiana, 1887, died in Georgetown on 5 December 1892. [F.7.677]

MUIR, JOHN, son of John Muir in Greenhall, died in Demerara on 5 August 1808. [SM#71.78]; his widow married Daniel Mackay in Santa Cruz, in Morningside, Edinburgh, on 17 February 1825. [BM#17.638]

MUIRHEAD, ARCHIBALD FOREMAN, a merchant in New Amsterdam, Guiana, died 19 April 1863. Cnf Edinburgh 1865

MUNRO, DUNCAN CAMERON, born 1819, H.M. Consul and Lloyd's shipping agent, died in Paramaribo, Surinam, on 5 February 1870. [S#8305]

MUNRO, GEORGE, settled in Berbice, father of George Munro a student at Marischal College, Aberdeen, in 1825. [AUL]

MUNRO, JAMES GORDON, son of James Gordon Munro, Saxe Coburg Place, Edinburgh, died in Georgetown, Demerara, 1851. [S.11.2.1852]

MUNRO, JAMES ST JOHN, HM Consul in Monte Video, cnf 1879 Edinburgh. [NAS.SC70.1.196/572]

MUNRO, KATIE JANE, daughter of Nicol Munro, married Charles Cumming Smith of Plantation Lochaber, in New Amsterdam, Berbice, on 27 August 1878. [S#10,999]

MUNRO, LOUISE CATHERINE, niece and adopted daughter of Mrs Munro, Viewfield House, Merchiston, Edinburgh, married James Alexander Bascom, at Plantation Success, Demerara, on 14 July 1881. [S#11,884]

MUNRO, R. F., born 1800, youngest son of D. Munro at Bridge of Alness, died on Foulis Plantation, Berbice, 15 July 1830. [S#1120]

MURDOCH, Captain ALEXANDER, born 1806, husband of Janet Wilson, died in Demerara 26 October 1839. [Greenock g/s]

MURDOCH, ALEXANDER, from Bellie, Banffshire, then in Essequibo, died 11 November 1840, cnf Edinburgh 1841

MURE, JAMES OCHTERLONY LOCKHART, born 1796, from Livingston, Kirkcudbright, died in Georgetown, Demerara, on 28 February 1863. [S#2431]

MURRAY, Reverend ARCHIBALD DOUGLAS, born 1826, minister of St Andrews, Georgetown, Demerara, died on 3 December 1863. [Wigtown g/s]; cnf 1864 Edinburgh. [NAS.SC70.1.120/530]

MURRAY, ALEXANDER JOHN, born 1813, second son of David Murray an accountant in Edinburgh, died in Berbice during August 1837. [AJ#4691]

MURRAY, JAMES, merchant in Demerara, co-owner of the Ocean of Greenock, 1799. [NAS.CE60.11.6/78]

MURRAY, JAMES, Demerara, educated at King's College, Aberdeen, from 1798 to 1801. [AUL]

MURRAY, JOHN, in Demerara, late in Portsoy, Banffshire, cnf 1795 Aberdeen.

MURRAY, WILLIAM, born 1842, son of James Murray in Slatehouse, Jedburgh, Roxburghshire, died in Callao on 18 March 1868. [S#7724]

MURRAY, Mrs, born 1816, from Wigtownshire, died in Buenos Ayres in 1871. [SRP#365]

MUSCHET, Dr GEORGE, in British Guina, youngest son of Richard Muschet a merchant in Dalkeith, Midlothian, died in St Kitts on 24 March 1860. [S#1517]

NAIRN, ROBERT, in Mompox, Columbia, 1825,
[NAS.SC58.59.10.118]; died 1 January 1827. Cnf Edinburgh
1830

NAYLOR, ..., son of John Edward Naylor, was born in Valparaiso
on 10 December 1877. [EC#29124]

NEILL, JOHN, son of John Neill a merchant in Glasgow, died in
Demerara on 15 March 1839. [SG#8/769]

NEILSON, DAVID, born 1870, son of Alexander Neilson and Mary
Russell, died in Rosario, South America, 13 April 1890.
[Renton Millburn g/s]

NEILSON, JOHN CAMPBELL, in Georgetown, Demerara, cnf 1885
Edinburgh. [NAS.SC70.1.238/140]

NEWELL, CHARLES BARBER, eldest son of James Newell of
Goldielea, Dumfries, died in Herrera, Zacatecas, Mexico, on
25 January 1872. [S#8947]

NEWELL, WILLIAM, in Zacaticas, Mexico, cnf 1876 Edinburgh.
[NAS.SC70.1.193/346]

NEWLANDS, LOUIS FRANCIS, married Maria Amelia de Jobim,
daughter of Jose Ferreira Porto, in Rio de Janeiro on 29
January 1877. [S#10,487]

NEWLANDS, THOMAS SCOTT, died in Rio de Janeiro on 8 April
1876. [S#10,219]

NEWLANDS, THOMAS SCOTT, jr., Rio de Janeiro, married
Margaret Othilia Schilling, daughter of Carol Jacob Schilling,
Porto Alegre, Brazil, there on 27 December 1879. [S#11,403]

NICHOLSON, FRANCIS MAXWELL, was born on 24 December
1855 in Pencaitland, Midlothian, son of the Reverend Maxwell
Nicholson and Frances Oliphant, a merchant in Buenos
Ayres. [F.1.116]

NICHOLSON, THOMAS WILLIAM, eldest son of J. W. Nicholson, a
farmer in Nisbet, East Lothian, died in Bahia Blanca, South
America, on 7 October 1884. [S#12906]

NICHOLSON, ..., daughter of James Nicholson, was born in
Monte Video on 4 March 1883. [S#12,397]

NICHOLSON, ..., son of James Nicholson, was born in
Valparaiso, Chile, on 1 May 1883. [S#12,422]

NICHOLSON, JOHN, a butcher in Kirkcaldy, Fife, emigrated to
South America in August 1899. [FH, 19.8.1899]

NICOL, A., from Kirkcaldy, emigrated to South America during February 1898. [FFP,12.2.1898]

NICOL, ANDREW, born 1876, son of Mr Nicol a confectioner in Linktown, settled in Punta Arenas, owner of the Imperial Hotel, died 27 January 1908. [FFP, 28.3.1908]

NICOL, JOHN, born in Leven, Fife, 1845, late of Aberdeen, died in [La Nora, Iquique, Chile,?] Lanariaqueque, Peru, on 7 May 1881. [St Nicholas g/s, Aberdeen][S#11,845]

NICOL, ..., son of James Watson Nicol, was born in Buenos Ayres on 27 February 1880. [S#11,426]

NICOL, ..., daughter of James Watson Nicol, was born in Chacomo, Buenos Ayres, on 14 August 1881. [S#11,940]

NICOLL, WILLIAM, born 1869, second son of George Nicoll, 1 Hunter Place, Aberdeen, died in Rio de Janeiro. [AJ: 11.2.1892]

NICOLSON, ..., daughter of James Nicolson of the River Plate Telegraph Company, died in Monte Video on 24 July 1879. [S#11,272]

NICOLSON, ERSKINA MCLEAN, infant daughter of James Nicolson, died in Monte Video on 24 April 1880. [S#11,501]

NICOLSON, JOHN, born 1819, an engineer late of the Fife and Kinross Railway, died in Arequipa, Peru, on 7 April 1881. [S#11,830]

NIMMO, JAMES, educated at St Andrews University, minister of St Luke's, British Guiana, 1868. [F.7.677]

NISBET, P., a planter in Aurora, Essequibo, 1802. [NAS.RD3.298.262; RD3.298.256]

NISBET, PETER, son of Peter Nisbet in Glasgow, died in Demerara on 12 August 1802. [SM#64.859]

NISBET, PETER, a merchant in Demerara ca.1806-1830. [NAS.CS234.seqn.34/17]

NIVEN, DANIEL, born 1837, died in Buenos Ayres on 28 November 1890. [Lochranza g/s]

NIVEN, HUGH, a merchant from Glasgow, died in Demerara during January 1803. [EEC#14299]

NORTON, ..., son of Robert Norton, was born in Tijuca, Rio de Janeiro, on 23 December 1877. [EC#29123]

OGILVIE, RACHEL, born in 1847, daughter of John Ogilvie in Dundee, and wife of James R. Balfour in Valparaiso, died in Arequipo, Peru, on 3 July 1878. [EC#29284/317][S#10,937]

OGILVIE, THOMAS, married Maria Constancia Frietus, daughter of the late Colonel Frietus, in Bahia on 17 December 1831. [GkAd#3818]

OGILVY, WILLIAM, second son of John Ogilvy of Inchewan, Angus, died on the Island of Ruatan, Bay of Honduras, on 14 February 1861. [S#1816]

OGILVY, ..., daughter of Thomas Ogilvy jr., was born in San Guillermo, Argentina, on 5 November 1873. [EC#27858]

OLIPHANT, JOHN, born in 1796 in Pittenweem, Fife, died in Demerara on 14 November 1850. [PR.11.1.1851]

ORR, THOMAS, born 1809, eldest son of Thomas Orr a timber merchant in Edinburgh, 'many years in Havannah, Cuba', died in New Orleans 10 June 1870. [S#8413]

OUGHTERSON, JOHN, died in Cordoba, Argentina, 1 October 1888, buried in San Geronimo cemetery. [Helensburgh g/s]

OUGHTERSON, JOHN, son of John Oughterson and Janet Robertson, died in Cordoba, Argentina, 1 October 1888. [Helensburgh g/s]

OUTRAM, JOSEPH, of Joseph Outram and Company in Tacna and Valparaiso, died in Tacna, Peru, on 21 November 1878. [EC#29457]

PAE, PETER, eldest son of David Pae, 17 St James terrace, Glasgow, died at Rio Blanca, Lima and Oraya Railway, Peru, on 30 October 1874. [S#9798]

PALMER, JOSEPH, born in Scotland, admitted as a member of the St Andrews Society of New York in 1815, a merchant in Lima, Peru, died in South America during 1827. [ANY.2.41]

PARISH, ..., daughter of Woodbine Parish, HM Consul General, was born in Buenos Ayres on 26 April 1828. [EA]

PARK, JAMES BRUNTON, from Edinburgh, married Henriettawidow of Pausto Masenelli of Liverpool, in Valparaiso on 4 March 1882. [S#12,103]

PARK, WILLIAM, born 1830 son of James Park in Ardrossan, Ayrshire, of Pasley, Templeton and Company, Glasgow and

Demerara, died in Georgetown, Demerara, on 30 August 1868. [S#7857]; cnf 1869 Edinburgh. [NAS.SC70.1.143/316]

PARKER, WILLIAM, a builder in Demerara, 14 February 1845. [NAS.RS.Edinburgh.53/281]

PATERSON, ALEXANDER, AM, MD, FRCSE, married Margaret Ann Andson, only daughter of James Andson in Arbroath, Angus, in Bahia, Brazil, 6 June 1871. [S#8714]

PATERSON, CHARLES AUSTIN, younger son of Alexander Paterson of Bahia, Brazil, died in Pernambuco, Brazil, on 29 June 1878. [S#10,909]

PATERSON, JEANIE GORDON, infant daughter of Dr J. L. Paterson, Boa Vista, Grange Loan, died in Bahia in 1879. [S#11,284]

PATERSON, JOHN DALGLEISH, of Christiansburgh, married Grace Edgar Lewis, daughter of Thomas Lewis, Parton, Kirkcudbrightshire, in Georgetown, Demerara, on 27 April 1860. [DC#23500]

PATERSON, JOHN LIGERTWOOD, in Bahia, Brazil, cnf 1883 Edinburgh. [NAS.SC70.1.225/723]

PATERSON,......, son of Alexander Paterson, MD, FRCSE, was born in Bahia, Brazil, on 17 April 1872. [S#8986]

PATERSON,......, son of William A. Paterson of Paterson and Henderson, and his wife daughter of William McLean in Granton, was born in Mexico on 3 November 1878. [S#11,038]

PATERSON,......, daughter of Dr J. L. Paterson, was born in Bahia, Brazil, on 24 July 1879. [S#11259]

PATON, EDWARD, born in Ancrum, Roxburghshire, on 5 December 1834, second son of Reverend John Paton, minister of Ancrum, and Mary Paton, a merchant in Pernambuco, Brazil. [F.2.101]; married Mary, eldest daughter of Henry Gibson in Pernambuca, there on 22 April 1869. [S#8054]

PATON, HENRY GIBSON, only child of Edward Paton, died in Pernambuco on 27 March 1871. [S#8629]

PATON, ..., son of Edward Paton, was born in Pernambuco on 28 January 1870. [S#8296]

PATON, ..., son of Edwaard Paton, was born in Pernambuco on 17 February 1876. [S#10,165]

PATON, ..., son of Edward Paton, was born in Pernambuco on 24 March 1882.[S#12,089]

PATTERSON, JAMES, a merchant in Givara, Cuba, died 7 June 1857. Cnf Edinburgh 1860

PATTERSON, ROBERT, in Demerara, father of John Winter Patterson born 1815 who was educated at Edinburgh Academy from 1824 to 1828. [EAR]

PATTERSON, ROBERT, a planter in Demerara, dead by 1830. [NAS.GD23.6.658]

PATTISON, EDWARD, a die maker at the Mint of Lima, married Carolina Juanita Maria, youngest daughter of Luis Francisco Vaslin, a merchant in Lima, on 5 February 1868. [S#7690]; late of Edinburgh, died in Lima, Peru, on 6 May 1868. [S#7761]; his wife died in Lima on 5 November 1868. [S#7919]

PAUL, JAMES, born 1832, son of John Paul, mason in Perth, and Catherine Whytock, died in Buenos Ayres, 12 December 1867. [Greyfriars g/s, Perth]

PEARSON, ADAM, from Glasgow, married Isabella Montgomerie, youngest daughter of William Montgomerie a farmer in Loudoun, Ayrshire, in Buenos Ayres on 1 March 1875. [EC#28251]

PEARSON, ISABEL, eldest daughter of John F. Pearson in Buenos Ayres, married Nicholas Isaac Huite-Bouwer of Amsterdam and Demerara, in Buenos Ayres on 16 March 1879. [EC#29514]

PEARSON, ..., daughter of Adam Pearson, was born in Demerara on 10 December 1838. [SG#8/740]

PEEBLES, CHARLES, a merchant in Valparaiso, cnf Edinburgh 1891. [NAS.SC70.1.295/689]

PEEBLES, JANE, born 1860, wife of Alexander Kennedy a merchant in Chanaral, Chile, lost in the Pacific Steam Navigation Company's steamer Atacama, off Caldera, Chile, on 30 November 1877. [S#10,762]

PEEBLES, ROBERT, eldest son of John Peebles in Ardgowan, Greenock, died in Rio de Janeiro on 20 Marc\h 1876. [S#10,222]

PENNY, ALEXANDER, second son of James Penny of Park, died in Oruro, Bolivia, on 17 January 1893. [AJ:28..2.1893]

PENNY, ANDREW, son of William Penny, bap. in Birse parish, Aberdeenshire, 17 May 1831, jumped ship at Arica, Chile, around 1853, later owner of the San Jose silver mine, Oruro, Bolivia, married Maria Galindo, died in Bolivia 1890.[AFHS#74/37]

PENNY, ROBERT H., born 1841, youngest son of John Penny in North Queensferry, Fife, died in Huanta, Peru, on 13 June 1880. [FJ]

PETER, M. LINDSAY, youngest son of the late John Peter of Kirkland, died at Sevigne near Buenos Ayres on 17 March 1882. [PJ]

PETER, ROBERT, with his wife, and children Sarah born 1817, James born 1820, and Helen born 1826, emigrated from Cromarty on the Planet of London, Captain William Barclay, on 1 October 1825, landed at La Guayra on 2 December 1825, settled at Topo, Columbia, by 1827. [PRO.FO.18/47; FO.199/3/32]

PHILIP, ALEXANDER BROCKIE, in Valparaiso, cnf Edinburgh 1897. [NAS,SC70.1.360/44]

PHILIPS, NEIL SMITH, born 1823, eldest son of Andrew Philips, Union Row, Aberdeen, died in Demerara on 13 December 1842. [AJ#4960]

PHILP, ANDREW KIRK, late of Kinmundy and Rora schools, eldest son of Robert Philp a saddler and ironmonger in Lochgelly, Fife, died in Oruro, Bolivia, on 29 September 1902. [DJ][AJ:3.10.1902]

PIERCE, Reverend W. E., drowned, with his wife, two daughters and a son, at Tabenetto Falls, British Guiana, 29 September 1881. [S#11,950]

PLAYFAIR, JAMES OCTAVIUS, born in 1839, son of George Playfair, died in Buenos Ayres on 19 August 1864. [St Andrews g/s, Fife]

PLAYFAIR, JESSIE, widow of Colonel Weston of the Bengal Army, died on Estancia d'Estonia, Salto, Uruguay, 21 February 1870. [S#8325]

PLAYFAIR, ROBERT HALDANE, born in 1836, son of William Davidson Playfair and Anne Ross, died in Buenos Ayres on 3 June 1865. [St Andrews g/s, Fife]; cnf 1866 Edinburgh. [NAS.SC70.1.19/93]

PLAYFAIR, WILLIAM, a planter in British Guina, cnf 1867 Edinburgh. [NAS.SC70.1.134/438]

POLLARD, WILLIAM BRANCH, born 1806, Auditor General of British Guiana, died in Georgetown, Demerara, on 9 December 1878. [S#11,077]

POLLOCK, DAVID, an engineer from Lanark and Glasgow, died at Rio Grande de Sol, Brazil, cnf Edinburgh 1890. [NAS.SC70.1.280/894]

POLLOCK, GRAY, born 18 June 1802, son of Reverend John Pollock and Margaret Dickson, died 25 June 1836 in Julapa, Mexico. [F.3.413][New Calton g/s, Edinburgh]

POLSON, SARAH, only daughter of John Polson in Old Aberdeen, married D. Melville a merchant in Berbice, in Old Aberdeen on 31 January 1828. [S#846.114]

POPE, WILLIAM, fourth son of James Pope a wine merchant in Leith, died in Monte Video on 13 July 1874. [S#9802]

PORTER, JAMES ROBERT, born 1839, died at Plantation Golden Fleece, Essequibo, British Guina, on 29 September 1876. [S#10,386]

PORTER, ROBERT, born 1868, eldest son of Andrew Porter from Kirkcaldy, died in Taltal, Chile, on 2 February 1891. [PJ]

PRENTICE, ALEXANDER, born 1825, son of J. Prentice and Isabel Stewart in Greenock, a civil engineer in Lima, Peru, died 1896. [Inverkip g/s, Renfrewshire]

PRETTIE, FRANCIS S., of the 76th Regiment, married Mary Rose, daughter of Peter Rose of Demerara, in Georgetown, Demerara, on 15 September 1838. [AJ#4746]

PRIMROSE, ARCHIBALD, died in Buenos Ayres during 1821. [S#224.143]

PRINGLE, WILLIAM, a planter in Surinam, 1675, 1676. [SPAWI.1675.401; 1676.943]

PRINGLE, WILLIAM, born 1791, son of John Pringle, a jeweller in Perth, and his wife Janet Cameron, died in Demerara in December 1815. [Greyfriars g/s, Perth]

PROCTOR, ISABELLA, eldest daughter of A. F. Proctor, Golden Square, Aberdeen, wife of Mariano Penny, died in Antofagasta, South America, on 17 May 1900. [AJ:19.5.1900]

PROUDFOOT, JOHN, from Glasgow, late of Monte Video and Rio Grande do Sol, died in Birkenhead, England, on 7 March 1875. [EC#28217]

PURVES, JAMES, a merchant in Valparaiso, married Jeannie Peters Burleigh, daughter of James Burleigh, La Noria, Iquique, in Valparaiso on 14 July 1881. [S#11,912]

PURVES, JAMES, in Valparaiso, cnf Edinburgh 1896. [NAS.SC70.1.351/365]

PURVES, PETER, born in Edinburgh 1838, locomotive superintendent of the Santiago and Valparaiso Railway, died in Valparaiso on 31 October 1878. [S#11,050]

PURVES, ..., daughter of Alexander Purves, was born at Santa Domingo Mines on 28 March 1876. [S#10,213]

PYPER, JAMES, born in 1840, youngest son of John Pyper, 106 King Street, Aberdeen, died in Georgetown, Demerara, on 1 September 1864. [AJ#6095]

RAE, JAMES, minister in British Guina 1893-1918. [F.7.677/680]

RAE, WILLIAM, son of William Rae in Aberdeen, educated at Marischal College, Aberdeen, from 1835 to 1839, graduated MA, later a teacher in Buenos Ayres and in Monte Video. [MCA#2.493]

RAEBURN, WILLIAM, born 1865, eldest son of Captain John Raeburn, 14 East Hermitage Place, Edinburgh, drowned at Port Oliva, South America, in 1881. [S#12,027]

RALPH, ..., daughter of Henry Fraser Ralph, was born in Valparaiso, Chile, on 2 June 1885. [S#13092]

RAMSAY, DAVID WILLIAM, in Charlottetown, Prince Edward Island, died in South America, cnf 1883 Edinburgh. [NAS.SC70.1.227/452]

RAMSAY, EBENEZER., in Buenos Ayres, son of Thomas Ramsay in Alloa, Clackmannanshire, married Charlotte Christina

McCallum, third daughter of Donald McCallum in Calcutta, in Monte Video on 4 October 1874. [EC#28124][S#9774]

RAMSAY, EBENEZER, in Monte Video, 13 January 1899. [NAS.RS.Edinburgh.202/258]

RAMSAY, GILBERT, born 1809, from Ayrshire, died in Buenos Ayres in 1871. [SRP#366]

RAMSAY, JAMES, son of Reverend James Ramsay in Glasgow, matriculated at Glasgow University in 1808, to Columbia by 1820, served in the Columbian Navy, killed 1826. [MAGU#7603]

RAMSAY, JOHN FRASER, son of Patrick Rigg Ramsay, died in South America during October 1873. [EC#27814]

RAMSAY, ROBERT, fourth son of Robert Ramsay a writer in Dumfries, died in Surinam on 24 April 1818. [BM#3.248]

RAMSAY, ..., daughter of Ebenezer Ramsay, was born in Monte Video on 10 December 1875. [S#10,137]

RAMSAY, ..., son of E. Ramsay, was born in Monte Video on 25 September 1877. [S#10,700]

RANKEN, GEORGE THOMAS, son of William Ranken, died at Golden Grove, Demerara, on 6 May 1840. [EEC#20071]

RANKEN, WILLIAM, MD, born 4 July 1794, settled in Demerara, died on 25 July 1867. [Sorn g/s, Ayrshire]

REID, ADAM, with his wife, and children Sarah born 1824, Joseph born 1825, and Simon Bolivar born 1827,emigrated from Cromarty on the Planet of London, Captain William Barclay, on 1 October 1825, landed at La Guayra on 2 December 1825, settled at Topo, Columbia, by 1827. [PRO.FO.18/47; FO.199/3/32]

REID, ALEXANDER, with his wife, and son John born 1825, emigrated from Cromarty on the Planet of London, Captain William Barclay, on 1 October 1825, landed at La Guayra on 2 December 1825, settled at Topo, Columbia, by 1827. [PRO.FO.18/47; FO.199/3/32]

REID, ALEXANDER, with his wife, and children John born 1807, Ronce born 1811, Alexander born 1814, Mary born 1818, and George born 1820, emigrated from Cromarty on the Planet of London, Captain William Barclay, on 1 October 1825, landed

at La Guayra on 2 December 1825, settled at Topo,
Columbia, by 1827. [PRO.FO.18/47; FO.199/3/32]

REID, DAVID, an engineer from Linktown, Kirkcaldy, Fife, then in
Rio de Janeiro, 1877. [NAS.RS,Kirkcaldy.17.104]

REID, DAVID, born 1840, died in Campos, Brazil, 8 August 1907.
[Kirkcaldy, Abbotshall, g/s]

REID, GEORGE, son of James Reid of Ardoch, died on Bellfield
Estate, Demerara, on 26 July 1819.]S#145.19]

REID, JAMES, Lieutenant of the Royal Navy, eldest son of James
Reid in Fraserburgh, Aberdeenshire, died in Buenos Ayres on
23 December 1819. [S.4.171]

REID, JAMES, a merchant in Lima, cnf 1866 Edinburgh.
[NAS.SC70.1.131/509]

REID, JOHN SHORT, elder son of Thomas Reid a solicitor and
banker in Moffat, Dumfries-shire, married Marion Bowie Scott,
eldest daughter of A. G. Scott of Glasgow and Valparaiso, in
Valparaiso on 27 July 1883. [S#12,540]

REID, ROBERT, born in Abbotshall, Fife, on 1 March 1836,
educated at St Andrews and at Edinburgh universities,
graduated MD, physician at the British Hospital in Buenos
Ayres in 1862, died 2 April 1870. [FH, 26.5.1870][Kirkcaldy,
Abbotshall, g/s]

REID, THOMAS, from Leith, Captain of the barque Aries, died in
Rio de Janeiro on 19 January 1868. [S#7665]

REID, Dr ...., born 1866, of the British Hospital, died in Buenos
Ayres on 2 April 1870. [S#8360]

REID, ..., daughter of James Reid, was born in Valparaiso on 26
February 1867. [S#7395]

RENNY, WILLIAM, in Belleville, Cordoba, Argentina, cnf Edinburgh
1898. [NAS.SC70.1.374/362]

REOCH, ANDREW, late of Demerara, died in Stirling, 1854.
[S.6.9.1854]

RHIND, JAMES, MD, married Juanita Valientes in Ascuncion,
Paraguay, 5 September 1867. [S#7639]; staff surgeon of the
Army of the republic of Paraguay, eldest son of W. Rhind a
banker in Stockport, died in Trinity, Ascuncion, Paraguay, on
1 October 1868, [S#7932]

RICHARDSON, G. A., in Demerara, graduated MD at King's College, Aberdeen, on 5 May 1823. [AUL]

RICHARDSON, W. B., manager of the New Quebrada Company Mines, married Gertrude L. Herman, in La Luz, Venezuela, on 12 December 1875. [EC#28178]

RICHARDSON, WILLIAM BROWN, born in 1840, youngest son of Francis and Christian Richardson in Edinburgh, died at Potosi Mines,Venezuela, on 18 February 1880. [Edinburgh, St Cuthbert's, g/s][S#11,429]

RICHARDSON, WILLIAM DUNN, a mining engineer in Potosi, Venezuela, cnf Edinburgh 1888. [NAS.SC70.1.266/368]

RICHARDSON, ..., daugher of Henry Graham Stewart Richardson, was born in Monte Mayo, Frayle Muerto, Argentina, on 8 October 1870. [S#8514]

RICKETTS, SAMUEL, second son of Samuel Ricketts a merchant in Surinam, educated at Glasgow University in 1816. [MAGU#291]

RICKETTS, THOMAS, eldest son of Samuel Ricketts a gentleman in Gloster, Surinam, educated at Glasgow University in 1815. [MAGU#291]

RINTOUL, GEORGE, second son of David Rintoul a farmer in Burnside, Kennoway, Fife, died in Callao, Peru, on 10 January 1885. [S#13007]

RITCHIE, DAVID, from Rio de Janeiro, married Jane Cromar, born 9 April 1830 daughter of Reverend Andrew Cromar and Jane Philip. [F.5.506]

RITCHIE, GEORGE, possibly from Elgin, Morayshire, in Barbados then in Demerara, died 1790. [NAS.CC8.8.128-2]

RITCHIE, THOMAS, a spirit dealer in Valparaiso, Chile, died 12 October 1842, cnf Edinburgh 1850

RITCHIE, WILLIAM WYSE, late a clothier in Glasgow and Edinburgh, died in Buenos Ayres on 5 May 1867. [S#7471]

RITCHIE, WILLIAM, minister of St Luke's, British Guiana, 1831-1837. [F.7.677]

RITCHIE, ..., daughter of James Ritchie, was born in Laranjeivas, Rio de Janeiro, on 31 August 1862. [S#2280]

ROBB, GEORGE, minister of St Marks, British Guiana, 1877-1879. [F.7.679]

ROBB, ..., daughter of George Robb, MA, was born in Rosario de Santa Fe, Argentina, on 17 December 1898. [S#17332]

ROBERTSON, ARCHIBALD, fifth son of Charles Robertson of Kindeace, died in Demerara during 1795. [SM#57.133]

ROBERTSON, CHARLES, minister in Buenos Ayres, 1884-1885. [F.7.683]

ROBERTSON, GEORGE J., of the firm of Don Pedro Lopez Gama Pagrica, died on the Peru between Panama and Callao on 30 March 1868. [S#7736]

ROBERTSON, HARRY, born in Kiltearn on 19 July 1776 son of Reverend Harry Robertson and Anne Forbes, died in Demerara during 1795. [F.7.43]

ROBERTSON, JAMES, a farmer in Buenos Ayres, cnf 1870 Edinburgh. [NAS.SC70.1.149/104]

ROBERTSON, JANET, wife of John Oughterson, died in Cordoba, Argentina, 1 October 1888. [Helensburgh g/s]

ROBERTSON, or PRESTON or VINES, JESSIE, in Monte Video, cnf 1875 Edinburgh. [NAS.SC70.1.175/6]

ROBERTSON, JOHN LESLIE, married Carolina Aurelia Melhada, daughter of Charles Melhada, in Belize on 17 February 1873. [S#9277]

ROBERTSON, JOHN PARISH, born in Roxburghshire, settled in Argentina during 1813, later in Monte Grande, Buenos Ayres, from 1825. [SRP#3]

ROBERTSON, PETER, born in 1818, son of W. Robertson a hat manufacturer in Paisley, died in Belize, Honduras, on 27 November 1838. [SG#8/742]

ROBERTSON, PETER, youngest son of John Robertson sr., a baker in Edinburgh, died in Valparaiso on 18 May 1876. [S#10,285]

ROBERTSON, WILLIAM, in Demerara, 1808. [NAS.CS17.1.27/301]

ROBERTSON, WILLIAM, a planter on Lejuan Island, Essequibo, 1812. [NAS.RD5.129.194]

ROBERTSON, WILLIAM B., late of 22 Middle Arthur Place, Edinburgh, son of James Robertson, in Gifford, East Lothian, died in Callao, Peru, on 2 October 1877. [S#10,709]

ROBERTSON, WILLIAM PARISH, born in Roxburghshire, settled in Argentina during 1813, later in Monte Grande, Buenos Ayres, from 1825. [SRP#3]

ROBERTSON, ..., son of William Parish Robertson junior, was born in Valparaiso on 17 December 1860. [S#1762]

ROBERTSON, ..., son of John Robertson, was born in Penambuco on 10 September 1871. [S#8819]

ROBERTSON,...., son of James Robertson, was born in Estancia del Tala, Uruguay, on 27 April 1877. [S#10,570]

ROBINSON, ANDREW HAY, son of Dr James Robinson in Demerara, died in Demerara during 1818. [S#139.19]

ROBINSON, JAMES, and his sister Charlotte, in Demerara 1801. [NAS.RD2.282.669]

ROBINSON, Dr JAMES, died in Demerara on 4 December 1808. [SM#71.238]

ROBINSON, JOHN, with his wife, and children Emelia born 1816, Eleanor born 1818, John born 1821, Elizabeth born 1823, and Joseph L. born 1827,emigrated from Cromarty on the Planet of London, Captain William Barclay, on 1 October 1825, landed at La Guayra on 2 December 1825, settled at Topo, Columbia, by 1827. [PRO.FO.18/47; FO.199/3/32]

ROBSON, JOHN, born in 1814, eldest son of Richard Robson in Glasgow, died in Lima on 16 March 1838. [SG#7/685]

RODGER, ALEXANDER, born in 1834, son of William Rodger and his wife Catherine Fleming, died in Demerara in January 1852. [Eastern Cemetery g/s, Dundee]

ROEDERER, SOPHIA, widow of Patrick Sandeman of the Observatory there, died in Georgetown, Demerara, 17 May 1871. [S#8697]

ROGER, HUGH, born 1786, died 1839 in Demerara. [St Andrew's Scots Church g/s, Demerara]

ROGER, MARGARET, eldest daughter of John Roger in Kinbroon, Rothienorman, Aberdeenshire, wife of John Bruce, died in Antofagasta on 11 March 1896. [AJ:16.3.1896]

RODGER, W. H., son of James Rodger and Bessie Halliday, settled in Buenos Ayres before 1879. [Dunnikier g/s, Fife]

ROGER, WILLIAM, son of James Roger a tailor in Mid Street, Pathhead, Fife, apprenticed to James Ireland an ironmonger in Kirkcaldy, emigrated to Buenos Ayres in 1870, a sheep farmer there, father of John McCrindle Roger. [FFP, 17.12.1910]

ROSE, ALEXANDER, a surgeon, son of John Rose the Customs Collector at Thurso, died in Berbice on 23 August 1802. [EA#4066.02]

ROSE, ALEXANDER, and his wife, emigrated from Cromarty on the Planet of London, Captain William Barclay, on 1 October 1825, landed at La Guayra on 2 December 1825, settled at Topo, Columbia, by 1827. [PRO.FO.18/47; FO.199/3/32]

ROSE, HARRIET, daughter of James Rose, the Deputy Clerk of Session in Edinburgh, died in Demerara on 16 September 1822. [BM#12.803]

ROSE, JAMES TAYLOR, Hacienda El Almedral, Pacasmeyo, Peru, cnf 1884 Edinburgh. [NAS.SC70.1.233/175]

ROSE, JOHN BARNET, in Demerara, died 26 March 1821. Cnf Edinburgh 1827

ROSE, JOHN EXLEY, eldest son of Neilson Rose of the Carron Company in Leith, died in Santarem, Brazil, 15 May 1872. [S#9032]

ROSE, PETER, born 1 January 1787, Manager of the Colonial Bank and a Member of the Court of Policy, died in Georgetown, Demerera, on 9 September 1819. [St George's Cathedral g/s, Georgetown, Demerara]

ROSE, ROBERT, son of John Rose of Ormly, died in Demerara on 11 January 1805. [SM#67.565]

ROSS, ANDREW, fourth son of Hugh Ross of Kerse, died in Berbice on 26 September 1820. [BM#8.482]

ROSS, ANGUS BETHUNE, born 1812, eldest son of Reverend Duncan Ross in Loth, Sutherlandshire, died on Plantation Penitence, Demerara, 9 June 1841. [AJ#4884]

ROSS, ANGUS, from Tain, then in Buenos Ayres, cnf Edinburgh 1893. [NAS.SC70.1.319/511]

ROSS, FRANCIS ALLAN, minister in British Guiana 1876-1892. [F.7.677]

ROSS, GEORGE, a magistrate in Demerara, son of Charles Ross a merchant in Aberdeen, 1843. [NAS.SH]

ROSS, HENRY CAMPBELL, of the London and Brazilian Bank, and son of William Ross, 15 Craigie Street, Aberdeen, died in Rio de Janeiro on 5 March 1892. [AJ:10.3.1892]

ROSS, ISABEL, daughter of David Ross HM Consul in Coquimbo, Chile, wife of Edward Squire of Copiapo, Chile, and of Swansea, Wales, died in childbirth 28 February 1860. [S#1516]

ROSS, JAMES, of A. Edwards and Co. in Valparaiso, died in Coquimbo, Chile, on 29 December 1867. [S#7761]

ROSS, JOHN, born around 1776, died in Nigg, Berbice, on 16 July 1807. [SM#68.958][DPCA#270]

ROSS, JOHN, superintendent and pastor of the Scots colony at Topo, Columbia, died at sea bound for Philadelphia in 1826

ROSS, PETER, in Demerara, 2 June 1820. [NAS.RGS#160/59]

ROSS, ROBERT, from Honduras, married Margaret Elizabeth, daughter of Alexander Mitchell of Garcrogo, at Troqueer Holm on 15 September 1813. [SM#75.799]

ROSS, of Skeldon, WILLIAM, a planter, son of Hugh Ross of Kerse, born in 1788, died in Berbice on 19 February 1840, cnf Edinburgh 1840. [Greyfriars g/s, Edinburgh] [NAS.SC70.1.60/4]

ROSS, WILLIAM, late of Berbice, later in Edinburgh, 1849. [NAS.RS38.GR2471/131]

ROSS, JOHN, son of David Ross MD, was born on Plantation Hazard, Nickerie, Dutch Guina, 27 September 1868; died there 11 September 1870. [S#7877/8491]

ROSS, ..., daughter of David Ross MD, was born in Nickerie, Dutch Guiana, 16 April 1870. [S#8359]

ROSS, ..., daughter of John W. Ross of Hacienda de San Ysodro, was born at Chihuahua, Mexico, on 7 January 1899. [S#17348]

ROWE, RALPH, born 1847, third son of William Hutton Rowe a surgeon in Coldstream, Berwickshire, died in Chillean, Chile, on 5 February 1869. [S#8009]

ROUGVIE, DAVID, a sugar planter in Matanzas, Cuba, 18 August 1882. [NAS.RS.Edinburgh.146/79]

RUCK, WALTER JAMES, born 1850, died in Rio de Janeiro on 4 March 1873. [S#9252]

RUNCIMAN, ALEXANDER EUING, youngest son of Reverend David Runciman, DD, Glasgow, died in Salta, Argentinia, on 29 August 1874. [S#9736]

RUNCIMAN, ELIZABETH ISABELLA, born in Edinburgh on 14 December 1855, daughter of Reverend David Runciman and Margaret Aitchison, married George O'Connell, died in Venado, Tuerto, Argentina, on 4 August 1918. [F.3.435]

RUNCIMAN, ROBERT INGLIS, born in Edinburgh on 9 April 1848, son of Reverend David Runciman and Margaret Aitchison, a merchant in Buenos Ayres. [F.3.435]; married Mary, daughter of Andrew Spring in Portland, Maine, in Buenos Ayres on 24 April 1876. [EC#28576][S#10,228]

RUNCIMAN, ..., son of Robert Inglis Runciman, was born in Buenos Ayres on 23 January 1877. [EC#28810][S#10,462]

RUSSELL, JAMES H. G., born in 1861, second son of Reverend John Russell in Grange, died in Leonora, Demerara, on 10 December 1885. [AJ:16.12.1885]

RUSSELL, JOHN, a merchant in Essequibo, died 4 January 1874, father of James Seward Russell in Glasgow. [NAS.SH.3.3.1886]

RUTHERFORD, EDWARD, MD [Edinburgh], Member of the Royal College of Surgeons, seventh son of the late Thomas Rutherford of Fannington, died in Cordova, Argentina, on 13 November 1870. [S#8569]

ST CLAIR, ISABELLA HOME, second daughter of Commander Charles St Clair RN, married Watkin W. Jones MD, in Georgetown, Demerara, on 2 August 1883. [S#12,520]

SANDEMAN, HUGH, born 1830, fourth son of Glas Sandeman and his wife Margaret Stewart of Bonskeid, Perthshire, died in Buenos Ayres on 20 December 1854. [EEC#22715][Perth, Greyfriars, g/s]

SANDEMAN, PATRICK, the Observatory, married Sophia Roderer, daughter of Dr Roderer of Demerara, in Georgetown, Demerara, on 13 October 1849. [SG#18/1868]

SANG, EDWARD, son of Walter Sang a nurseryman in Kirkcaldy, Fife, an engineer who died in Callao on 13 March 1869. [FH][S#8024]

SANGSTER, ...,son of William S. Sangster, was born in Lima on 28 March 1877. [EC#28914]

SAUNDERS, FRANCIS WILLIAM, a merchant in St Luis Potosi, Mexico, cnf 1886 Edinburgh. [NAS.SC70.1.252/249]

SAWERS, ..., son of James Sawers, was born in Valparaiso on 21 July 1867. [S#7527]

SAWERS, ..., son of John Sawers, was born in Valparaiso on 3 September 1873. [S#9408]

SCOBIE, ANGUS, son of Kenneth Scobie in Achmore, Assynt, died in Demerara on 11 December 1807. [SM#70.398]

SCOTS, ..., daughter of Dr Scots, was born in Georgetown, Demerara, in 1868. [S#7796]

SCOTT, DAVID, born 1848, son of David Scott and Margaret Ritchie, died at Mazatlan, Mexico, 24 November 1878. [Girvan g/s]

SCOTT, JAMES, born in Kinclaven, Perthshire, on 14 October 1792, son of Reverend John Scott and Ann Swan, Captain of the British Legion in Columbian Service, killed at the Battle of Carabobo in South America on 24 June 1821. [F.4.163]

SCOTT, JAMES HARPER, born 1857, died in Origaba, Mexico, on 20 March 1888. [Greenlaw, Berwickshire, g/s]

SCOTT, JOHN, in Demerara, son of John Scott a merchant and Elizabeth Buchanan in Kincardine on Forth, 1802. [NAS.RD3.295.657]

SCOTT, JOHN, in Buenos Ayres, 1850. [NAS.RD5.853.449/453]

SCOTT, MARION BOWIE, eldest daughter of A. G. Scott of Glasgow and Valparaiso, married John Short Reid, elder son of Thomas Reid a solicitor and banker in Moffat, Dumfries-shire, in Valparaiso on 27 July 1883. [S#12,540]

SCOTT, PHILIP, born 1861, eldest son of Philip Scott a carpenter in Buckhaven, Fife, died at the British Hospital, Esquina, Buenos Ayres, on 15 December 1888. [FFP]

SCOTT, STEPHEN, MD, son of the late John Scott a farmer in Limpitlaw, Kelso, Roxburghshire, died in Georgetown, Demerara, on 19 March 1872. [S#8961]

SCOTT, WILLIAM, born 1856, eldest son of James Scott, Links, Kirkcaldy, Fife, emigrated to Kingston, Jamaica, in 1875, then

to Belize, British Honduras, died there on 6 February 1877.
[FFP, 24.3.1877][S#10,504]

SCOTT, WILLIAM, son of John Scott in Renfrewshire, matriculated
at Glasgow University in 1830, settled in Valparaiso, died in
London on 28 February 1892. [MAGU#12622]

SCOTT, WILLIAM, born 1833, an engineer from Kirkcaldy, Fife,
settled in Valparaiso by 1866, died there on 1 December
1884. [FH]

SCOTT, Mrs, wife of Reverend James Scott, late of Peterhead,
Aberdeenshire, died in Demerara on 12 January 1836.
[AJ#4596]

SEDGELY, Captain JOHN R., son of Mrs Sedgely in Broughty
Ferry, died in Valparaiso on 1 May 1851. [FJ#969]

SELKRIG, ROBERT, late of Demerara, died in Edinburgh on 5
March 1823. [SM#111.520]

SEMPLE, ROBERT, from Demerara, married Adriana, daughter of
William Moore in St Eustatia, in Glasgow on 30 September
1817. [BM#2.126]

SHAND, GEORGE, in Demerara, later in Aberdeen, husband of
Mary Walker, cnf 1793 Aberdeen

SHANKLIE, PETER, late of Leith Walk Nursey, Edinburgh, died on
Estancia de San Jorge, 1853. [S.26.10.1853]

SHANTY, R., born 1851, from Glasgow, died in Buenos Ayres in
1871. [SRP#366]

SHARP, EDWARD, married Christian Clerk Campbell, daughter of
T. Campbell of the General Post Office in Edinburgh, in Monte
Video during 1872. [S#8963]

SHAW, EDWARD, late in Demerara then in Inverness, 1833.
[NAS.RS.Inverness#136]

SHAW, JAMES, in Lima, cnf 1880 Edinburgh.
[NAS.SC70.1.202/316]

SHAW, JAMES, an engineer in Iqique, Chile, cnf 1886 Edinburgh.
[NAS.SC70.1.247/316]

SHAW, ..., son of Walter Shaw, was born in Callao, Peru, on 1
December 1877. [EC#29122]

SHEARER, PETER, born 1831, son of Donald Shearer [1785-
1844], died in Panama 27 May 1854. [Dundee g/s]

SHEPHERD, JOHN, born 1861, son of David Shepherd in Boarhills, St Andrews, Fife, died in Bahia, Brazil, on 26 July 1878. [PJ]

SHEPPARD, JOHN, born 1833, youngest son of John Sheppard and Alison Darey, George Street, Edinburgh, died on Estancia Puntas de Maciel, near Monte Video on 1 November 1868. [Edinburgh, St Cuthbert's, g/s][S#8065]

SHIACH, DAVID, born 1817, son of William Shiach and Christian Torrie, died in Paramibo, Surinam, on 24 March 1846. [Rothes g/s]

SHIRREFFS, LAUDERDALE, born 1837, died in Demerara during 1854. [Banchory Ternan g/s]

SHORT, JOHN REID, in Monte Video, Uruguay, by 1899, nephew of John Short Reid who died 31 December 1841, and grandson of Walter Reid, a writer in Leith, and his wife Joanna Short who died 30 May 1851. [NAS.SH.10.8.1899]

SIM, ANDREW, born in Ellon, Aberdeenshire, a planter, died on the Garden of Eden Plantation, Demerara, on 7 August 1821. [BM#10.609][S.5.257]

SIME, ALEXANDER, born in 1839 son of William Sime, died in Lambayeque, Peru, on 20 May 1901. [Dundee, Western, g/s]

SIME, CRAWFORD, son of William Sime [1797-1863], died in Rio de Janeiro aged 21. [Dundee, Western, g/s]

SIME, JAMES PULLAR, a merchant in Iquique, married Jessie Robertson Craig, second daughter of John H. Craig a merchant in Huases, in Valparaiso on 16 March 1876. [EC#28600]

SIME, JAMES PULLAR, born 1841, son of William Sime, died in Invique, Chile, on 22 October 1898. [Dundee, Western, g/s]

SIMSON, ALEXANDER, born 1802, minister of St Mark's, British Guiana, 1826-1830, died in September 1830. [F.7.679]

SIMPSON, ANDREW, fourth son of Andrew Simpson, Evandale, St Quivox, educated at Glasgow University in 1811, died in Demerara during 1820. [MAGU#255]

SIMPSON, Mrs CATHERINE, widow of Admiral Simpson of the Chilean Navy, died in Valparaiso on 9 May 1879. [EC#29568]

SIMPSON, CHARLES, born 1865, eldest son of Charles Simpson a blacksmith in Leven, Fife, died in Buenos Ayres on 5 July 1887. [FFP]

SIMPSON, JAMES, born 1818, youngest son of Captain Alexander Simpson, died in Demerara on 4 July 1833. [SG#2/174]

SIMSON, JOHN, in Demerara, 1814. [NAS.RD5.182.697]

SIMPSON, JOHN, born during 1829, son of James Simpson and Margaret Milne in Banff, a shipmaster, died in Demerara in August 1867. [Banff g/s]

SIMSON, JOHN, eldest son of Thomas Simson of Blainchie, died in Buenos Ayres on 28 April 1871. [S#8664]

SIMPSON, JOHN, born 1843, died in Buenos Ayres in 1871. [SRP#365]

SIMPSON, JOHN, born 1812, formerly in Limekilns, master of the barque Majorian, a shipowner who died in Georgetown, Demerara, 17 December 1880. [Greyfriars g/s, Perth] [S#11,699]

SIMPSON, RICHARD, born in 1873, youngest son of William Simpson, dairyman, Gladstone Terrace, Woodside, Aberdeen, died in Pernambuco, Brazil, on 24 November 1889. [AJ:14.12.1889]

SIMPSON, ..., in Demerara in 1830. [NAS.GD23.6.658]

SIMS, WILLIAM, in San Juan, Cuba, died 21 March 1860. Cnf Edinburgh 1862

SIMSON, Reverend A. G., born 1802, died 1830 in Demerara. [St Andrew's Scots Church g/s, Demerara]

SIMPSON, or MACNEE, Mrs JEANNIE WILLIAMINA, sometime in Glasgow then in Calle Gaute, Mexico, cnf Edinburgh 1900. [NAS.SC70.1.391/899]

SIMSON, JOHN, born 1782, Collector of Rum Duties in Demerara and Essequibo, died in Inverness 4 June 1843. [Urquhart g/s]

SINCLAIR, JAMES, born 1859, son of Alexander Sinclair a blacksmith of Albany Street, Kirkcaldy, Fife, a fireman who was killed in a locomotive accident in Chile during 1880, [DJ, 3.4.1880]

SINCLAIR, JAMES, born 1860, son of Alexander Sinclair late in Dunfermline, died in Malvoe, Chile, on 27 January 1881. [PJ]

SINCLAIR, JANE, daughter of John Sinclair in North Leith, married James Downie, an engineer, in Valparaiso on 6 August 1862. [S#2276]

SINCLAIR, JOHN O., San Salvador, son of George M. Sinclair, and grandson of John Strachan, died in Panama 9 January 1867. [S#7339]

SINCLAIR, NEIL, son of Archibald Sinclair [1775-1848] and Margaret McIntyre [1791-1850] in Greenock, a plumber, died in Mexico on 25 December 1884. [Greenock g/s]

SINCLAIR, THOMAS, from Leith, married Jessie Glass Gow, daughter of James Gow in Edinburgh, in Valparaiso on 25 November 1870. [S#8583]

SINCLAIR,......, son of Thomas Sinclair, was born in Valparaiso on 25 September 1871. [S#8831]

SKAKLE, JOHN, born 1844, chief officer of the Kiltearn of Liverpool, son of John Skakle a jeweller in St Nicholas Street, Aberdeen, died in Georgetown, Demerara, on 22 July 1865. [AJ:6.9.1865]

SKENE, WILLIAM, son of William Skene, (died 1856) a carpenter, and Isabella MacLoorie (1786-1834) in Taymouth, Perthshire, died in Belize, Honduras, during 1848. [Kenmore g/s, Perthshire]

SKINNER, GEORGE URE, born 1805, second son of Very Reverend John Skinner, Dean of Dunkeld and Dunblane, settled in Guatamala, died in Aspinwall, Panama, on 9 February 1862. [AJ#6215][S#7342]

SKINNER, THOMAS, born 1842, son of Alexander Skinner and Mary Bonthron in Kirkcaldy, Fife, died in Pisagua, Chile, on 8 October 1912. [FFP]

SKIRVING, GEORGE, a merchant from Monktonhall, emigrated to Buenos Ayres in 1812, moved to Valparaiso, Chile, drowned off Isle de los Chios on 22 March 1825. [DPCA#1215]

SIMPSON, CATHERINE, widow of Admiral Simpson of the Chilean Navy, died in Valparaiso on 9 May 1879. [EC#299568]

SLATER, Reverend THOMAS, born 1829, died 1905 in Demerara. [St Andrew's Scots Church g/s, Demerara]

SLATER, WALTER, infant son of Reverend Thomas Slater the minister of St Andrew's, died in Georgetown, Demerara, on 23 August 1873. [S#9406]

SMALL, CHARLES JOHN, in Plantation Middenburg, Demerara, cnf 1884 Edinburgh. [NAS.SC70.1.237/480]

SMALL, GAFFER, in Demerara, cnf 1880 Edinburgh.
[NAS.SC70.1.202/202]

SMALL, HENRY, from Dundee, died in Omoa, Brazil, on 13 August
1848. [AJ#5158]

SMART, JAMES, a printer, 166 Calle San Martin, Buenos Ayres, 1
June 1903. [NAS.RS.Forfar.66/30]

SMART, ROBERT, printer's assistant, 166 Calle, San Martin,
Buenos Ayres, 1903. [NAS.RS.Forfar.66.30]

SMELLIE, ARCHIBALD O. S., born 1873, died 1904 in Demerara.
[St Andrew's Scots Church g/s, Demerara]

SMELLIE, JAMES, son of Reverend James Smellie, St Andrew's,
Orkney, died in Georgetown, Demerara, on 26 April 1883.
[S#12,445]

SMITH, ADAM, a merchant and advocate in Demerara, died on 14
December 1812, son of William Smith an advocate in
Aberdeen (1722-1793) and Margaret Skene (1744-1796), [St
Nicholas g/s, Aberdeen]; cnf 1813 Edinburgh.
[NAS.SC70.1.10/314; CC8.8.140]

SMITH, ALEXANDER, born in 1836, an engineer, son of Peter
Smith a stonecutter in Aberdeen, married Jane Cameron,
eldest daughter of David Cameron an ironfounder in Bahia, in
HM Consulate there on 5 December 1863, died in Bahia,
Brazil, on 2 December 1872. [AJ#6053][EC#27535]

SMITH, CHARLES CUMMING, Plantation Lochaber, married Katie
Jane Munro, daughter of Nicol Munro, in New Amsterdam,
Berbice, on 27 August 1878. [S#10,999]

SMITH, GEORGE, a clerk in Pinra, Peru, cnf Edinburgh 1891.
[NAS.SC70.1.291/977]

SMITH, JAMES, born in Fowlis Wester, Perthshire, during 1825,
son of Thomas Smith a tailor, educated at Glasgow
University, a minister in Argentina from 1850, died on 9
October 1906. [F.7.683]

SMITH, JESSIE LEE, infant daughter of C. Cumming Smith, Pin,
Haarlem, Demerara, died at Pin, Rose Hall, Berbice, on 20
March 1881. [S#11,768]

SMITH, JOHN, in Berbice, son of Thomas Smith and Janet Frew in
Bathgate, West Lothian, 1815. [NAS.RD5.160.367]

SMITH, JOHN, a surgeon, died in Berbice on 14 December 1822. [SM#91.519]

SMITH, JOHN, born in 1840, son of William D. Smith and Janet Morrison in Burntisland, died on Plantation Waterloo, Nickerie, Surinam, on 16 May 1872. [Burntisland g/s, Fife][S#9014]

SMITH, JOHN WEIR, son of Andrew Smith, Boat of Ashogle, Turriff, Aberdeenshire, died in Pernambuco, Brazil, on 24 November 1889. [AJ:14.12.1889]

SMITH, ROBERT ANDERSON, born in 1834, son of John Smith, 1801-1861, and his wife Amelia Smith, 1793-1879, died in Bahia on 2 June 1855. [Arbroath Abbey g/s, Angus]

SMITH, ROBERT, a planter in Demerara, 1888. [NAS.SC58.42.56.1011]

SMITH, THOMAS, in Valparaiso, cnf 1877 Edinburgh. [NAS.SC70.1.184/173]

SMITH, WILLIAM, born 1810 in Aberdeen, son of John Smith and Margaret Bowman, a merchant who died in Bahia 2 July 1852. [Brechin Cathedral g/s, Angus]

SMITH, WILLIAM GIBSON, second son of James Smith in Birkhill, Lesmahagow, Lanarkshire, sometime farmer in Kilbucho, Peebles-shire, and his wife Helen Watt Brown, third daughter of David Brown in Rowhead, Biggar, Lanarkshire, were murdered by guachos at La Victoria, Tandil, Buenos Ayres, on 1 January 1872. [S#8910]

SMYTHE, GEORGE PETRIE, born 1845, second son of Henry Smythe late schoolmaster in Scoonie, Fife, died in Callao on 11 March 1874. [FH][EC#27934][S#9586]

SMYTHE, WILLIAM HENRY, of the Callao Dock Company, son of Henry Smythe a teacher in Leven, Fife, married Maggie C. Elliot, younger daughter of Captain Elliot in Valparaiso, in Lima on 21 August 1879. [S#11,305]

SMYTHE, ..., son of William H. Smythe, of the Callao Dock Company, late of Leven, Fife, was born in Callao, Peru, on 25 August 1881. [S#11,923]

SOMMERS, FRANCIS, of Sommers and Ewing in Rio de Janeiro, drowned in the River Plate on 17 September 1817. [BM#2.607]

SOMERVILLE, JAMES, born in St Boswells, son of Reverend Robert Somerville and Constantia Williamson, settled in Buenos Ayres. [F#2/193]

SOUTHWELL, CHARLES, of the Mint of Lima, married Andrea Leonica daughter of Luis Francisco Vaslin, a merchant in Lima, on 5 February 1868. [S#7690]

SPEEDIE, ..., son of William Speedie, was born in Mollendo, Peru, on 21 August 1872. [S#9108]

SPENCE, DAVID, from Upper Scappa, Orkney, then in Demerara, cnf 1885 Edinburgh. [NAS.SC70.1.241/855]

SPENCE, ..., son of Charles Spence, was born in Rio de Janeiro on 30 March 1830. [PA#46]

SPIERS, AMY MARIA, youngest daughter of John Spiers in Glasgow, married Charles Herald, second son of Joseph Herald, Monton Bank, Manchester, in Monte Video on 2 October 1874. [S#9766]

SPINK, JAMES, born 1832 son of William Spink and Elizabeth Gordon, died in Rio de Janeiro on 2 February 1853. [Arbroath Abbey g/s]

SPRATT, G., from Wigtownshire, died in Buenos Ayres in 1871. [SRP#365]

SPROAT, SAMUEL, in Demerara, before 1813. [NAS.SH.3.5.1813]

STEDMAN, Captain JOHN GABRIEL, an officer of the Scots Brigade in the Netherlands, later a soldier in Dutch Guina, author of 'Narrative of a Five Years Expedition' [London, 1806] [NAS.GD99.229.9/2]

STEELE, ALEXANDER, son of William Stele [died 1848] and Helen Stronar [died 1873], died in Bahia June 1853. [Arbirlot g/s]

STEELE, WILLIAM, a planter in Demerara, will, 1782. [NAS.GD1.470.1]

STEELE, ..., son of John Steele, was born in Rio de Janeiro on 28 July 1877. [S#10,643]

STENHOUSE, JAMES ROY, a clerk in Rosario Santa Fe, cnf Edinburgh 1891. [NAS.SC70.1.296/403]

STENHOUSE, THOMAS, son of Alexander Stenhouse in Edinburgh, drowned in the Black River, Poyais, on 12 November 1823. [S#428.103]

STEPHEN, WILLIAM, born 1889, son of William Stephen (1863-1911), died at Port Concepcion, South America, 5 February 1912. [Bressay, Shetland, g/s]

STEPHENSON, DAVID, fifth son of Andrew Stephenson in Glasgow, died in Valparaiso during an earthquake on 19 November 1822. [S#367.456]

STEVENSON, DAVID, son of David Stevenson of Rio de Janeiro and Glasgow, died in Rio de Janeiro, 1852. [S.28.7.1852]

STEVENSON, HENRY CUNARD, born 1838, died 1876 in Demerara. [St Andrew's Scots Church g/s, Demerara]

STEVENSON, HUGH, a merchant in Peru, nephew of Margaret Maule in Edinburgh, 1853. [NAS.SH]

STEVENSON, JOHN, born in Melrose, Roxburghshire, the proprietor of the *Guina Chronicle* of Georgetown, Demerara, was drowned in the Orinocco River on 25 August 1823. [BM#15.492]

STEVENSON, MARJORY, youngest daughter of Robert Stevenson a farmer in Auchanachie, Banffshire, married David Morn, from Glasgow, in the British Consulate, Mexico City, 1856. [CM#21776]

STEWART, ALEXANDER, late of Lusignan, Georgetown, Demerara, then in Edinburgh, 1866. [NAS.RS.Inverness#282]

STEWART, DAVID, second son of David Stewart, 14 Waterloo Place, Edinburgh, died in Mexico during 1828. [S#885.426]

STEWART, DONALD, minister of St Mark's, British Guiana, 1831. [F.7.678]

STEWART, HERIOT, late in Limekilns, Fife, died in Tampico, South America, on 27 May 1869. [PJ][S#8088]

STEWART, JAMES, second son of James Stewart of Persie, residing in Dowally, Perthshire, died in Valparaiso on 11 April 1822. [S#311.7][DPCA#1066]

STEWART, JAMES, a merchant in Mexico before 1851. [NAS.SH.23.9.1851]

STEWART, JAMES, born 1841, died in Buenos Ayres in 1871. [SRP#365]

STEWART, JAMES STIRLING, at Estancia La Lila, Concordia Entre Rios, Argentina, son of James Stewart of Blackhouse who died 28 May 1895, possibly from Largs, Ayrshire. [NAS.SH.114.5.1897]

STEWART, JAMES engineer in Demerara, cnf 1879 Edinburgh. [NAS.SC70.1.193/638]

TAYLOR, DAVID K., born 1865, a plumber in Dunfermline, third son of James Taylor, 55 Hutcheson Street, Glasgow, died in the British Hospital, Buenos Ayres, on 21 February 1890. [DJ]

TAYLOR, GEORGE, born in Inverurie Aberdeenshire, during 1831, died in New Amsterdam, Berbice, Demerara, on 28 September 1860. [AJ:7.11.1860]

TAYLOR, JOHN, in Progresso, South America, cnf Edinburgh 1891. [NAS.SC70.1.293/866]

TAYLOR, Captain THOMAS, born in 1799, died in Bahia on 19 March 1850. [Anstruther Easter g/s, Fife]

TAYLOR, THOMAS EDWARD, minister in Buenos Ayres in 1894-1895. [F.7.683]

TAYLOR, WILLIAM BRACEY, inValparaiso, grandson of Helen Howie or Taylor in Stonehaven, Kincardineshire, who died 2 December 1866. [NAS.SH.18.2.1897]

TAYLOR, WILLIAM CONNON, born in 1853, eldest son of John Taylor, 216 King Street, Aberdeen, died on Plantation Great Diamond, Demerara, in February 1885. [AJ:2.3.1885]

TELFER, ALEXANDER, late in Demerara, died in Glasgow on 27 February 1834. [SG#2/225]

TELFER, WILLIAM, in Demerara, cnf 1834 Edinburgh. [NAS.SC70.1.49/858]

TEVIOTDALE, JAMES RAMSAY JEFFERSON, son of David Teviotdale, a skipper from Monifieth in Angus, and his wife Eliza Jefferson who were married in Arbroath on 6 June 1863, was born on 9 April 1867 aboard the brig Sunnyside in Valparaiso Bay. [NRH/MRB]

THOM, JOHN ALFRED, a clerk in Brazil, grandson of William Ferguson, a coal-merchant in Greenock, Renfrewshire, who died on 24 March 1841. [NAS.SH]

THOMAS, ALFRED, MB, CM Edinburgh 1869, son of F. Thomas in Blackburn, died in Monte Video 3 may 1870. [S#8361]

THOMSON, ALEXANDER, born in 1854, youngest son of John Thomson in Aberdeen, died in Georgetown, Demerara, on 19 September 1881. [AJ]

THOMSON, GEORGE, third son of George Thomson, The Elms, Stirling, died in Pernambuco on 6 February 1873. [S#9237]

THOMPSON, GEORGE, agent for the Pacific Steam Navigation Company in Coquimbo, Chile, died in Dumfries, cnf 1899 Edinburgh. [NAS.SC70.1.384/638]

THOMPSON, J., born 1839, from Edinburgh, died in Buenos Ayres in 1871. [SRP#366]

THOMSON, JAMES R., superintendent engineer of the Pacific Steam Navigation Company, married Mary, only daughter of John Menzies of Chucuito, Calloa, in Lima on 29 June 1877. [EC#28954] [S#10,605]

THOMSON, JAMES, an engineer in Campos, Rio de Janeiro, 1883. [NAS.RS.Kirkcaldy.22.57]

THOMSON, JOHN, eldest son of John Thomson, 26 Nelson Street, Edinburgh, married Jessie Ramsay, eldest daughter of Gilbert Ramsay, formerly of Ayrshire, in Buenos Ayres on 5 March 1862. [S#2147]; eldest son of John Thomson, Duncan Street, Edinburgh, died in Buenos Ayres on 16 April 1871. [S#8684]

THOMSON, ROBERT, a surgeon, second son of Thomas Thomson the town clerk of Musselburgh, Midlothian, died in Demerara during February 1821. [BM#9.245]

THOMSON, THOMAS, an overseer, son of Alexander Thomson a tobacconist in Edinburgh, died on Plantation Plaisance on the east coast of Demerara on 2 May 1824. [DPCA#1146]

THOMSON, THOMAS, MD, born in Hamilton, Lanarkshire, during 1803, drowned in the Pomeroon River on 3 June 1827. [S#789.488]

THOMSON, THOMAS YULE, born 1847, a baker from 41 Broughton Street, Edinburgh, died in Callao on 14 January 1869. [S#8029]

THOMSON, ..., son of John Thomson, was born in Buenos Ayres on 5 February 1863. [S#2430]

TODHUNTER, GEORGE BORTHWICK, infant son of George Borthwick and Jane Graham, died in Salto, Band Oriental, on 20 November 1874. [AO]

TONNER, EDWARD, a deep sea pilot, son of James Tonner a general dealer in Annan, Dumfries-shire, died in Rosario 5 November 1882. [AO:5.1.1883]

TORRANCE, JOHN, born 1848, son of John Torrance, draper in Cumnock, [1809-1864], died in Lima, Peru, on 8 July 1893. [Old Cumnock g/s]

TOWNS, JOHN, born 1818, son of John Towns and Helen Kier, died in Pernambuco 1850. [Arbroath Abbey g/s, Angus]

TRAILL, WILLIAM, eldest son of William Traill of Gifford, died in Cayenne on 26 October 1876. [S#10,415]

TROTTER, ..., daughter of A. B. Trotter in Georgetown, Demerara, was born aboard the R.M.S. Neva on 14 October 1868. [S#7879]

TROTTER, ..., , son of A. B. Trotter, was born at Clifton House, Georgetown, Demerara, on 11 June 1877. [S#10,603]

TROTTER, ALLAN BOWIE, youngest son of George Trotter a builder in Edinburgh, died in Georgetown, Demerara, on 3 March 1885. [S#13021]

TUCKER, JOHN, born 1838, son of Nathaniel Tucker [1810-1881] and Jane Tucker [1825-1889], died in Valparaiso on 28 January 1854. [Greenock g/s]

TULLOCH, HENRY, a merchant in Demerara, 1806. [NAS.AC7.77]

TURCAN, WILLIAM, born in 1826, son of George Turcan and Agnes Mercer, died in Rio de Janeiro on 2 March 1852. [Tulliallan g/s]

TURNBULL, ADAM, from Edinburgh, died in Mexico 25 January 1867. [S#7358]

TURNBULL, Mrs, from Fochabers, Morayshire, died in Demerara on 1 February 1801. [GC #1519]

TURNER, JAMES, son of Coll James Turner, died 1837 in Demerara. [St Andrew's Scots Church g/s, Demerara]

TURNER, WILLIAM GEORGE, born 1843, youngest son of James Turner, schoolmaster in Abbotshall, Fife, died in Chascomas, Buenos Ayres, on 10 September 1866. [FA]

TWEEDIE, WILLIAM, an engineer with Imperial Brazilian Collieries, eldest son of ..... Tweedie a publisher in London, married Alice Anne Philips, youngest daughter of Reverend Thomas

Philips, at Rio Grande, Brazil, on 29 November 1872.
[EC#27543]

TYNDALL, SAMUEL, in Berbice, graduated MD at Edinburgh University in 1819. [EUL]

TYRE, JAMES GEORGE, a bank clerk from Glasgow, died in Buenos Ayres, cnf Edinburgh 1901. [NAS.SC70.1.400/30]

URQUHART, Colonel C. G., eldest son of David Urquhart of Braelongwell, Governor of Carabusa, died on 3 March 1828. [EA]

VALENTINE, GEORGE, born in 1844, an engineer, second son of John Valentine, farmer in the Mains of Loirston, Nigg, Kincardineshire, died in Peru on 14 July 1883. [AJ:18.9.1883]

VALLANCE, THOMAS DRYBURGH, son of Reverend Vallance of Tinwald, Dumfries-shire, died in Buenos Ayres on 4 March 1874. [AO]

VIRTUE, JOHN, a chemist, married Maggie, third daughter of David Pollock in Stirling, in Georgetown, Demerara, 10 October 1870. [S#8545]

WALKER, ALEXANDER WALES, MD, born 1831, of St Clement's Street, Aberdeen, died in Pernambuco on 15 May 1862. [AJ#5971]

WALKER, ALEXANDER, born 1845, son of William Walker, Thistle Street, Burntisland, Fife, died in Santiago, South America, on 15 December 1873. [S#9528]

WALKER, GEORGE ROBERT, from Dunfermline, son of Dr Walker in Woodcot, Dollar, died in Buenos Ayres on 28 March 1871. [FH][S#8675]

WALKER, JAMES FIFE, born on 3 February 1814, son of Reverend Alexander Walker and Elizabeth Grant in the parish of Urquhart, Morayshire, a planter in Berbice who died on 6 August 1842. [F.6.411]

WALKER, JAMES, born in 1833, a manufacturing chemist from Glasgow, died in San Antonio, Peru, on 8 January 1875. [EC#28213]

WALKER, JOHN, in Honduras, married Katherine May Ann Lindsay Robertson, sixth daughter of Major Robertson of Craig, at Craig House, Perthshire, on 1 July 1851. [AJ#5400]

WALKER, THOMAS, born 1855, a boiler maker, second son of John Walker a pilot in Kirkcaldy, Fife, died in Callao, Peru, on 24 September 1883. [PJ]

WALKER, WILLIAM, born on 19 October 1809, son of Reverend Alexander Walker and Elizabeth Grant in Urquhart, a planter in Berbice, died there on 25 April 1843. [F.6.411]

WALKER, WILLIAM, born 1856, eldest son of William Walker a farmer in Nigg, Kincardineshire, died in Belize, British Honduras, 2 November 1883. [Banchory Devenick g/s] [AJ:27.11.1883]

WALKER, ..., daughter of Melville A, Walker late Captain of the 78th Highlanders, was born in Monte Video on 17 December 1867. [S#7650]

WALKINGSHAW, ROBERT, at Rancho del Oro, Mexico. 1827. [NAS.SH.30.8.1827]

WALKINGSHAW, ROBERT, in Mexico 1846. [NAS.SH.16.11.1846]

WALKINGSHAW, ROBERT, born in 1847, second son of Robert Walkingshaw in Glasgow, died in Buenos Ayres on 8 August 1875. [EC#288382]

WALLACE, GEORGE, with his wife, and children John born 1813, Donald born 1815, Hugh born 1818, and Alexander born 1822, emigrated from Cromarty on the Planet of London, Captain William Barclay, on 1 October 1825, landed at La Guayra on 2 December 1825, settled at Topo, Columbia, by 1827, then emigrated to Guelph, Canada. [PRO.FO.18/47; FO.199/3/32]

WALLACE, JAMES BELL, born in Portmoak, Kinross, 11 April 1858, son of Alexander Wallace, a farmer, and Christina Greig, educated at St Andrews University, MA 1883, minister of St Luke's, British Guiana, 1893-1921, died 7 August 1921. [F.7.677]

WALLACE, THOMAS, born in 1794, son of William and Esther Wallace, died in the Amazon River on 12 October 1863. [St Andrews g/s, Fife]

WALLACE, Dr WILLIAM, on the Three Friends Plantation(?), died in Demerara on 2 November 1823. [BM#15.249]

WALLIS, JAMES, born in 1823, son of William Wallis in Gartly, a minister in Demerara from 1854 to 1864. [F.6.42; 7.677]

WARDLAW, WILLIAM, born 1824, Lieutenant of <u>HMS Racer,</u> killed on the River Plate in 1846. [Dean Cemetery g/s, Edinburgh]
WATLINGTON, ..., son of V. V. Watlington, M.D., was born in Arecibo, Puerto Rico, on 5 April 1876. [S#10,253]
WATSON, ALEXANDER, son of Alexander Watson writer in Montrose, Angus, died at Laguia de Termines on the Gulf of Mexico, on 4 July 1839. [AJ#4786]
WATSON, JAMES, born 1868, son of Thomas Watson gas manager, dieed at Copiapo, Chile, 12 February 1876. [S#10,202]
WATSON, MARY ANN, youngest daughter of Captain James Watson, RN, Portsoy, Banffshire, married Hugh Watson, in Demerara on 27 January 1844. [AJ#5021]
WATSON, ..., son of Thomas Watson, was born in Copiapo, Chile, on 20 June 1875. [EC#28353]
WATT, JAMES, born in 1847, son of John Watt of Meathie and Isabella   Stormonth, died in Pernambico on 6 January 1884. [St Andrews Cathedral g/s, Fife]
WATT, JOHN, of Meathie, in Argentina 1867. [NAS.RS.Forfar.23.164]
WATT, ..., son of John A. Watt of Meathie, Angus, was born at Estancia la Maya, Frayle Muerto, on 16 April 1872. [S#9000]
WEATHERHEAD, ..., son of Reverend R. J. Weatherhead MA, British Chaplain, was born in Callao, Peru, on 25 May 1875. [EC#28314]
WEBSTER, JOHN, born in 1840, eldest son of John Webster at Bridge of Dee, Aberdeenshire, of Hopkins and Webster engineers, died in Bahia on 7 December 1875. [EC#28503][S#10,153]
WEBSTER, ..., son of Charles Henry Webster, was born in the Alexandra Colony, Argentina, on 7 January 1879. [EC#29479]
WEDDERSPOON, THOMAS COVENTRY, son of W. Wedderspoon in Perth, matriculated at Glasgow University 1837, a Commission Agent in Valparaiso and San Francisco, died 18 February 1905. [MAGU#14586]
WEIR, DANIEL, a merchant, son of Thomas Weir of Kerse, died in Demerara during 1793. [SM#55.153]

WEIR, DANIEL, a merchant in Buenos Ayres, died in Mendoza on 25 August 1824. [DPCA#1170]

WEIR, THOMAS DUNCAN, graduated B.Sc. from Glasgow University in 1881, a civil engineer in Caracas, Venezuela, [RGG.637]

WEIR, WILLIAM, graduated MD from Glasgow University in 1864, later in Sabara, Brazil, and Buenos Ayres. [RGG.638]

WEIR, ..., daughter of William Weir MD, was born at Rua de Sao Francisco, Sabara, Brazil, 7 January 1871. [S#8622]

WELLS, ANDREW, from Edinburgh, died in Monte Video on 25 March 1867. [S#7413]

WESTLAND, DAVID DOUGLAS, a civil engineer from Edinburgh, then in Salina, Cruz, Mexico, cnf Edinburgh 1900. [NAS.SC70.1.396/348]

WHITE, JAMES, born 1801, a farmer, with his wife Margaret, emigrated from Leith to Argentina on the Symmetry, master William Cochrane, on 22 May 1825. [SRP#18]

WHITE, MARGARET, in Buenos Ayres, married Lieutenant James Thorburn of the Royal Navy, in Buenos Ayres on 21 December 1847. [SG#17/1698]

WHITE, WILLIAM, born 1803, a farmer, with his wife Janet and a child, emigrated from Leith to Argentina on the Symmetry, master William Cochrane, on 22 May 1825. [SRP#18]

WHYTE, ANDREW, born 1847, son of Robert Whyte in Glasgow, died in Para on 6 December 1874. [S#9798]

WHYTE, HENRY ADAM, born 1852, son of Robert Whyte in Glasgow, died in Para on 6 December 1874. [S#9798]

WHYTE, THOMAS, born 1849, son of Robert Whyte in Glasgow, died in Pernambuco on 12 December 1874. [S#9798]

WHYTE, ..., sister of the late Bain Whyte, Writer to the Signet, widow of Ewan McLaurin, Charleston, America, died in Demerara on 29 December 1822. [SM#91.519]

WHYTE,......, daughter of John Whyte, was born at 49 Rua de Humalta, near Rio de Janeiro on 20 August 1877. [S#10,638]

WHYTE, ..., son of John Whyte, was born at Tijuca, Rio de Janeiro, on 6 March 1881. [S#11,747]

WHITELAW, JAMES, born in 1822, son of Alexander Whitelaw a surgeon in Kilmarnock, Ayrshire, and Mary Bell, died in Valparaiso on 15 July 1867. [Kilmarnock g/s]

WHITSON, ..., son of Archibald Whitson from Edinburgh, died in Calleo on 18 June 1870. [S#8422]

WHYTE, ..., son of John Whyte, was born in Boa Vista, Rio de Janeiro, on 17 August 1884. [S#12827]

WILKIE, ALEXANDER, a seaman, second son of James Wilkie a shoemaker in Kirkcaldy, Fife, died in Coquimbo on 6 August 1872. [S#9113]

WILLIAMS, FRANK, died in Santos, Brazil, on 20 October 1883. [S#12,606]

WILLIAMS, WILLIAM ALEXANDER, late of Calcutta, died in Buenos Ayres during 1817. [S#15.17]

WILLIAMSON, ALEXANDER, married Henrietta, daughter of Mr Hume a land surveyor in Belize, there on 6 August 1868. [S#7847]

WILLIAMSON, ARCHIBALD, married Mary Helena, eldest daughter of Charles B. Krabbe, a merchant, in Buenos Ayres on 13 March 1867. [S#7414]

WILLIAMSON, MARGARET, born in 1831, wife of Daniel Stewart, died in Acapulco, Mexico, 3 September 1853. [Kirkcaldy, Abbotshall, g/s]

WILLIAMSON, WILLIAM, in Demerara, cnf 1824 Edinburgh. [NAS.SC70.1.31/338]

WILLIAMSON, Dr .... emigrated from Cromarty on the Planet of London, Captain William Barclay, on 1 October 1825, landed at La Guayra on 2 December 1825, later returned to Britain

WILLIAMSON, ..., daughter of Archibald Williamson, was born at Waterloo, Quinta, Buenos Ayres, 6 June 1870. [S#8418]

WILLIAMSON, ..., daughter of Archibald Williamson, was born at Waterloo, Quinta, Buenos Ayres, 15 January 1872. [S#8914]

WILLIAMSON, ..., daughter of A. Williamson, was born in Buenos Ayres on 10 March 1874. [S#9608]

WILLIAMSON, ..., daughter of A. Williamson, was born at Waterloo, Quinta, Buenos Ayres, on 6 July 1876. [S#10,313]

WILLIAMSON,........, daughter of Alexander Williamson, was born in Belize, British Honduras, on 12 February 1877. [S#10,503]

WILLIAMSON, ..., daughter of A. Williamson, was born in Waterloo, Quinta, Buenos Ayres, on 8 March 1878. [S#10,836]

WILLIAMSON,....., daughter of Alexander WSilliamson, was born in Belize, Honduras, on 30 September 1878. [S#11,023]

WILSON, ANDREW, born in 1820, son of James Wilson and Elizabeth Whyte, died in Demerara on 19 April 1856. [Newburgh g/s, Fife]

WILSON, ANDREW, from Leith, died in Valparaiso on 19 February 1863. [S#2456]

WILSON, AUGUSTUS FORBES, minister of St Luke's, British Guiana, 1879. [F.7.677]

WILSON, GEORGE JAMES, in San Fernando, Buenos Ayres, nephew of Mary Ann Wilson or McDowell at the Kirk of Mochrum who died 16 February 1882. [NAS.SH..25.5.1897]

WILSON, JANET, born 1813, wife of Captain Alexander Murdoch, died in Demerara 10 October 1839. [Greenock g/s]

WILSON, JOHN, a merchant skipper based in Lima, Peru, settled in Santa Barbara, California, during the 1830s. [SHR#153/138]

WILSON, JOHN, born 1838, son of James Wilson in Edinburgh, died on <u>HMS Camelon</u> in Valparaiso 15 November 1870. [S#8558]

WILSON, JOHN, born in 1828, son of George Wilson and Janet Livingston, died in Buenos Ayres on 14 March 1895. [Mochrum g/s, Wigtownshire]

WILSON, ROBERT SMITH, second son of James Wilson a manufacturer in Earlston, Berwickshire, died in Havanna April 1873. [S#9315]

WILSON, ROBERT, born in 1849, eldest son of William Wilson in Strathaven, Lanarkshire, died in Rio de Janeiro on 11 April 1877.[EC#28891]

WILSON, Captain ROBERT, born 1850, died in Rio de Janeiro on 7 April 1894. [Dean g/s, Edinburgh]

WILSON, THOMAS, Golfdown Street, Dunfermline, an ironfounder in Valparaiso, Chile, from around 1869 to 1884, died in Minnesota, USA, on 11 April 1887. [DJ, 7.5.1887]

WILSON, WILLIAM, son of Thomas Wilson a writer in Edinburgh, died in Surinam on 6 August 1812. [SM#74.886]

WINGATE, GEORGE, son of John Wingate a manufacturer in Glasgow, died in Rio de Janeiro on 23 January 1821. [S#224.143]

WINNING, ISAAC, graduated MA from Glasgow University, a teacher at Mackay and Sutherland's English School in Valparaiso, in Chile. [RGG.655]

WOOD, Mrs BRIJIDA LYNCH, born 1854, wife of James S. Wood, died in Iquiqui, Chile, on 11 December 1898. [S#17348]

WOOD, JAMES GARDINER, Bote Mining Company, Zacatacas, Mexico. Cnf 1899 Edinburgh. [NAS.SC70.1.383/205]

WOOD, MARY FRASER, wife of William M. McCulloch, died in Georgetown, Demerara, on 3 September 1882. [S#12,224]

WRIGHT, HUGH, died in Paramaribo, Surinam, on 26 September 1877. [S#10,677]; cnf 1878 Edinburgh. [NAS.SC70.1.189/337]

WRIGHT, ..., daughter of John M. Wright, was born in Rosario de Sante Fe on 22 July 1869. [S#8127]

WRIGHT, ..., daughter of John M. Wright, was born at 75 Calle de Buenos Ayres, Rosario de Sante Fe, Argentina, on 5 April 1871. [S#8127]

WRIGHT, ..., daughter of John M. Wright, was born at 75 Calle de Buenos Ayres, Rosario de Sante Fe, Argentina, on 18 June 1873. [S#9368]

WRIGHT, ..., daughter of Percival C. Wright, was born in Pernambuca on 25 May 1879. [EC#29560]

WYLIE, JOHN, merchant in Bahia, Buenos Ayres and Rio de Janeiro, 1809-1820. [GUL]

WYLIE, JOHN, of Wylie, Cooke and Company, San Luis Potosi, Mexico, 1830-1840. [GUL]

WYLIE, ROBERT C., born in Hazelbank on 13 October 1798, second son of Alexander Wylie (1762-1840) a farmer in Dunlop, Ayrshire, and Janet Creighton (1766-1847), educated at Glasgow University in 1810, a ships surgeon then a physician and merchant in Mazathon, Mexico, later British Vice Consul in Honululu 1844-1845, Secretary of State for the Sandwich Islands, died in Honululu in 1865. [MAGU#259] [Dunlop g/s]

WYLIE, ROBERT, in Coquimbo, South America, licentate of the Royal College of Surgeons in 1809, graduated MD from Marischal College, Aberdeen, on 31 March 1820. [AUL]

YOUNG, AMELIA, daughter of William Young, married Commander Thomas Maitland of the Royal Navy, in Rio de Janeiro on 17 February 1828. [S#869.298]

YOUNG, FRANCIS, in Honduras, graduated MD from Edinburgh University in 1820. [EUL]

YOUNG, JAMES, born in Dundee during 1800, son of George Young, a weaver, and Mary Young, educated at St Andrews University, a minister in British Guina from 1841 to 1844, died in Broughty Ferry on 3 November 1882. [F.7.676]

YOUNG, JAMES, a minister in Callao, Peru, from 1858. [F#7.684]

YOUNG, JAMES, born 1838, second son of James Young in Methven, Perthshire, died in Demerara in 1867 on board the Cycla. [S#7515]

YOUNG, JOHN, jr., in Honduras, son of John Young a baker in Burntisland, Fife, and Christian Wild, 1804. [NAS.RD5.121.282]

YOUNG, Dr JOHN, in Belize 1850. [NAS.RD5.848.376]; died in Belize, British Honduras, 26 June 1862. [S#2236]

YOUNG, RODERICK, from Demerara, married Jessie, eldest daughter of Captain Mackay of Skail, in Inverness on 20 June 1810. [SM#73.553]; marriage contract, Roderick Young, Cuminsburgh, Demerara, and Janet or Jessie Mackay, daughter of William Mackay in Skail, Farr, Sutherland, 19 June 1811. [NAS.RD3.345.165]

YOUNG, ..., son of Roderick Young in Demerara, was born in Skerray on 3 May 1812. [SM#73.558]

YOUNG, THOMAS, late of Howie and Young, Whitebank Ironworks, Kirkcaldy, died in Lebu, Chile, on 15 March 1891. [FH]

YOUNGER, ANDREW, son of John Younger a shipowner in Leven, Fife, died in Buenos Ayres during June 1837. Cnf Edinburgh 1837

YOUNGER, ANDREW, born 1820, son of John Younger [1775-1842] and Margaret Horne [1790-1839] in Scoonie, Fife, died in Buenos Ayres 24 December 1844. [Scoonie g/s]

YOUNGER, JOHN, born during 1837, son of George Younger [1790-1853], a brewer in Alloa, and Jane Hunter [1792-...], died in Buenos Ayres in 1865. [SNQ.III.136]

YOUNGER, THOMAS BROWN, youngest son of Thomas Younger in Leven, Fife, married Frances Jane Roger, eldest daughter of Francis Younger in London, in Georgetown, Demerara, on 11 April 1878. [FH]

YOUNGER, ..., daughter of Thomas B. Younger, was born in Georgetown, Demerara, on 9 September 1883. [S#12,561]

YOUNGER, ..., daughter of John W.Younger, was born in Georgetown, Demerara, on 19 November 1883. [S#12,613]

REFERENCES

ARCHIVES

AUL = Aberdeen University Library, Scotland
BMu = British Museum, London
EUL = Edinburgh University Library, Scotland
GUL = Glasgow University Library, Scotland
NAS = National Archives of Scotland, Edinburgh
NLS = National Library of Scotland, Edinburgh
PRO = Public Record Office, London

PUBLICATIONS

AFHS= Aberdeen Family History Society journal, series
AJ = Aberdeen Journal, series
ANY = Biographical Register of St Andrews Society of New York
AO = Annandale Observer, series
BM = Blackwood's Edinburgh Magazine, series
CM = Caledonian Mercury, series
DC = Daily Courant, Edinburgh. series
DJ = Dunfermline Journal, series
DPCA= Dundee, Perth and Cupar Advertiser, series
EA = Edinburgh Advertiser, series
EAR = Edinburgh Academy Register
EC = Edinburgh Courant, series
EEC = Edinburgh Evening Courant, series
EFR = East Fife Recorder, series
F = Fasti Ecclesiae Scoticanae, J.Scott, [Edinburgh 1915]
FFP = Fife Free Press, series
FH = Fife Herald, series
FJ = Fife Journal, series
GC = Glasgow Courant, series
GH = Glasgow Herald, series

GkAd=	Greenock Advertiser, series
GM =	Gentleman's Magazine, series
GSP =	Glasgow Saturday Post, series
HMC =	Historical Manuscripts Commission, series
KCA =	Officers and Graduates of King's College P. J. Anderson,[Aberdeen 1893]
MAGU=	Matriculation Albums of Glasgow University, 1727-1858, W. I. Addison, [Glasgow 1913]
MCA =	Records of Marischal College, P. J. Anderson, [Aberdeen,1898]
PJ =	People's Journal, series
PR =	Pittenweem Register, series
RGG =	Register of Graduates of Glasgow University, 1727 -1898, W. I. Anderson, [Glasgow, 1898]
S =	Scotsman, series
ScG =	Scottish Genealogist, series
SG =	Scottish Guardian, series
SHR =	Scottish Historical Review, series
SM =	Scots Magazine, series
SNQ =	Scottish Notes and Queries, series
SRP =	Scots on the River Plate,
TMG =	The McClellans in Galloway, D. R. Torrance, [Edinburgh, 1996]
W =	Witness, series